NREMT Exam Prep
2019-2020

A Study Guide including 220 Test Questions and Answers for the EMT Basic Exam (National Registry of Emergency Medical Technicians)

Table of Contents

Chapter 8: Patient Care During an Emergency............ 55

Chapter 1: About the NREMT Exam

NREMT stands for National Registry of Emergency Medical Technicians. The NREMT exam is United States-based, and the equivalent of an EMT or emergency medical technician in some other countries is a paramedic or ambulance technician. These are terms typically used to refer to personnel offering health care on an emergency basis. Accreditation for the NREMT is under the United States National Commission of Certifying Agencies, which means that whatever exam the registry formulates meets the expectations and standards as set within the country's Standards for Education and Psychological Testing.

Emergency medical technicians are clinicians who have undergone training that prepares them to be able to respond fast when emergencies of a medical nature arise, or when there are people with injuries resulting from trauma or accidents. In many cases, EMTs offer ambulance services while under the employment of the government, hospitals or private firms. They are also employed by fire departments and police departments.

Ordinarily in every setup where EMTs are working, there is a physician acting as their supervisor; usually in the capacity of medical director. Still, there are trained EMTs who work on a voluntary basis, and these are often found in areas that are remote and far from specialized medical services.

How to Acquire Certification as an EMT

The National Highway Traffic Safety Administration (NHTSA) establishes the standards to be met by the institutions creating the curriculum as well as setting and grading the relevant exams, which comprise mainly the NREMT and those states that opt to conduct their own certification.

EMT Exam by States & NREMT Exam

There are 46 U.S. states that rely on the NREMT exam to identify competent EMTs for work within their jurisdictions, but others prefer to create their own exam and do the certification themselves. Either way, the exam must meet the requirements set by the NHTSA.

To be well prepared for either the NREMT exam or EMT exam, one needs to know the relevant material and the basic requirements. The information and techniques explained in this book are based on the NREMT exam, which is a Computer Adaptive Test (CAT).

Still, considering all EMTs must be well equipped with knowledge and skills as outlined by the NHTSA, the book will be of benefit to all candidates preparing for the EMT exam whether established by an individual state or the NREMT. The candidates seeking to take a state set exam can then contact their local Emergency Medical Services (EMS) office to see if there are any modalities specific to that state.

When it comes to qualifying as an Emergency Medical Technician, the NHTSA has identified four categories for recognition, each at its own level. You can choose to be an Emergency Medical Responder (EMR), an Emergency Medical Technician (EMT), an Advanced Emergency Medical Technician (AEMT), or a paramedic.

A Little History of the NREMT

The NREMT was established in 1970 when then-U.S. President Lyndon Johnson set up a committee to seek ways of standardizing emergency medical technician training. The president was specifically interested in enhancing traffic safety on highways. EMTs are expected to provide basic life support (BLS) during emergencies as well as stabilize and transport victims, who are sometimes in critical condition, to medical facilities.

Conditions to Qualify for NREMT Certification

You must be at least 18 years old to take the NREMT exam and be certified, although there are a couple of states that permit 16- and 17-year-olds to complete the exam.

To qualify for certification, a person must have passed the exam within the last two years.

Training Requirements for EMTs

Becoming an EMS requires a minimum of 40 to 80 hours of formal training, whereas EMT training is usually 120 to 180 hours. Advanced EMTs generally require 200 to 500 hours of formal training, and paramedics require 1,000 hours to 1,800 hours, or even more.

Besides those training hours, EMTs are required to undergo continuing education to maintain their certification. For the NREMT certification in particular, EMTs must complete a minimum of 48 hours of continuing education. Alternatively, they may complete a 24-hour refresher course.

Job Prospects & Wages for EMTs

Certified EMTs can work in many settings, and there is usually no shortage of job opportunities. They can work in pre-hospital medical services like EMS, fire departments and even with police agencies. EMTs are hired to work in entertainment settings and specific industries. Sometimes they may be called upon to render medical services even in non-emergency situations.

In 2016, government statistics showed 248,000 EMT jobs. As of May 2017, the median wage for an EMT on an annual basis was $33,380, and job opportunities are on the rise. Job opportunities for both EMTs and paramedics are projected to increase by 15 percent by 2026.

This projection takes into account the fact that emergencies such as road accidents involving vehicles, natural catastrophes and violence perpetrated by people, will never cease to occur.

The academic requirements for becoming an EMT or paramedic are not very stringent, as one only needs to complete a high school education and the NREMT exam plus the required continuing education after the initial certification. In fact, unlike some exams in the medical field, the NREMT exam requires no prior on-the-job experience. No previous medical experience is necessary to take the test.

Medical Categories EMT Candidates are Tested On

As has already been mentioned, EMTs' main responsibility is to provide basic life support to people who have been injured or are facing emergencies. As such, the areas that are tested involve a wide range of emergencies.

These areas include airways, cardiology, trauma, medical and general operational procedures. If you are well prepared in these five broad areas, you are well on the way to passing your NREMT exam.

Qualifying as a certified EMT serves as a strong foundation for building a career in a medical-related field. Not only do many EMTs end up becoming paramedics, but a good number move on to become nurses or doctors.

In Preparation for the Exam

It is important to establish a timeline before you register for the NREMT exam, so you can ensure you have fulfilled the requirements prior to the exam. For one, before you can schedule an examination date, you need to have been registered as a candidate by the NREMT. You also can't register until you have your letter of authorization, which grants you the go-ahead to take the exam.

You will receive a notification letting you know whether you are eligible for the NREMT exam, and before you take the exam you must pay a fee.

Candidates are advised to check their letters of authorization carefully once they receive them, to make certain the details contained therein are accurate. In case there are mistakes in your letter, get in touch with the national registry at (614) 888-4484.

Important Exam Details

In the NREMT exam, you should anticipate questions with four multiple-choice answers. Usually these questions will have been created by a committee of 10 to 20 experts.

Even as the experts concur on the correct answer for each question, they also ensure that the options that are incorrect have some degree of plausibility. Moreover, the experts ensure the questions are derived from sources that are commonly used as resource materials when teaching courses related to EMS.

About NREMT Exam Fees

As a candidate, you are expected to pay for the NREMT exam online, and this should be done via the NREMT website after you have registered and signed into your account.

Acceptable modes of payment include credit cards or school payment vouchers. You are also allowed to send your payment by mail, although this may cause you significant delay because you can't schedule your exam until your payment has cleared.

Chances of Retaking the NREMT Exam

If you take the NREMT exam and do not pass, you have a chance for a retake after 14 days. According to the examination body, candidates need these two weeks to prepare for the next attempt.

You can tell if you have officially passed or failed an exam within one or two business days of taking the test. The exam results are posted on the NREMT website, so you can log onto www.nremt.org to check yours.

How to Prepare Effectively for the NREMT Exam

According to successful EMTs, paramedics and other authorities, to prepare well for the NREMT exam you need to carefully study the materials used for the EMT course. One advantage they cite is the richness those materials have on the required basics.

These materials emphasize the importance of knowing CPR and shock treatment, and all other parts covered in the NREMT exam. You need to be familiar with airway and ventilation as well as oxygenation, trauma, all aspects of cardiology-related emergencies, medical emergencies and the operational procedures involved.

You also need to know key details for each of those areas, such as the airway's main components and what is considered a normal range when it comes to adult and pediatric respiration. It is also crucial that you understand emergencies of a diabetic nature, plus the different syncope causes.

Generally, around 15 percent of all the NREMT questions are about pediatrics, while around 85 percent of them are adult-related. This is generally the ratio across the five main categories tested. One thing that candidates often ignore when preparing for the exam is that the operational procedures section is a big part of the test. It is, therefore, important that you understand how, for instance, the National Incident Management System (NIMS) and the Incident Command System (ICS) work.

If you understand how the two systems operate and how to apply them in a situation of mass casualty, you will be at a greater advantage than many candidates who do not understand these operations that gained prominence after Sept. 11, 2001.

How to Be Prepared on Exam Day

You need to arrive early to sign in at the examination center. Otherwise, the stress of being late might be a distraction when you need to be very focused. This means you need to locate your exam center a day or more before the date of the exam and establish the quickest way of getting there.

Remember to bring two types of identification, one with a photo to confirm that you are the actual registered candidate. One of those IDs is left behind whenever you exit the exam room, such as to visit the bathroom, and you take the other ID with you to be used when you check back in.

Take some pencils with you in case you want to jot anything down. The exam center provides scrap paper. If you use this, you will need to turn it in along with the exam paper at the end of the session.

How to Tackle NREMT Exam Questions

The computer-based exam does not allow you to skip a question and return to it later. This means you have to deal with each question as it appears, whether you feel confident about your answer or not. The exam is set up this way so that each question builds on the next. If your answer shows you are not well versed on a topic, the next question is likely to be relatively simple and worth less points, whereas if your answer indicates a good knowledge of a topic, the question that follows is likely to be a little tougher and worth more. That way some candidates end up tackling fewer questions than others, as the system has the capacity to determine with 95 percent accuracy how well versed you are in the knowledge and skills being tested.

Questions Requiring Extra Attention

There is a way of telling when you are dealing with a question that calls for special attention. Look for qualifiers such as 'except' and 'always,' or 'never' and 'most suitable.' This means you need to take your time and read the question slowly and carefully.

Avoid Looking at the Answers First

It is advisable that you begin by reading each question in its entirety, and then try to determine your answer *without* initially checking the answer options provided. The reason is that by checking the answers before you finish reading the question, your response may be influenced by some of the answers given, and the option you pick may not be correct.

NREMT Questions

Each question has four answer options, all of them potentially correct. Since each choice is designed to have has some degree of plausibility, you may be confused if you aren't well prepared or don't carefully consider each answer. Your job is to choose the best or 'most correct' of all the choices.

Don't look too deep into a question—many questions are testing you on the basics. Imagining hidden complexities may just derail you.

Since 2018, the exam includes a calculator that appears on your screen. Use it to do the basic calculations required in some questions.

As long as you have prepared for the exam and follow these simple tips, you have a great chance of passing the NREMT exam with relative ease. Stay calm throughout the test by taking deep breaths whenever you find yourself a little nervous.

Chapter 2: Journey to Becoming an EMT

As an EMT, you will be expected to provide efficient, immediate help to patients who are either ill or injured away from conventional medical care and facilities. As such, it will generally be upon you to assess the health of patients and perform appropriate medical procedures like CPR, bleeding control, shock management, ventilation and immobilization. You will also be expected to handle transportation of patients to a medical facility.

In many instances, EMTs are dispatched to the emergency scene by a 911 operator, sometimes due to a car crash, a heart attack, a woman in labor, gunshot wounds, etc.

What Happens After a 911 Call

Once EMTs receive a 911 call from the dispatcher on duty or any other call, they are supposed to immediately drive to the scene by ambulance. Nevertheless, even though speed is of the essence, EMTs are expected to observe safety on the road and ensure they do not endanger other road users even during poor weather conditions. In short, EMTs are expected to be able to operate an ambulance with great skill and efficiency.

What EMTs do on Arrival at the Emergency Scene

Once at the scene of the emergency, EMTs are expected to check the environment for safety, assess the number of injured people, assess the patients' condition and then try to determine if patients have pre-existing health conditions. These steps help to determine whether the EMTs need to call for backup. Only after these preliminaries can the EMTs proceed to offer the emergency support required, following medical protocols and existing guidelines.

After EMTs open patients' airways as necessary, control bleeding, etc. they assess patients to see if they need additional assistance. Such additional help may include administering medication or oxygen, giving oral glucose or administering activated charcoal to mitigate the effects of poisoning.

How to Handle Patient Transportation

Ordinarily, EMTs work within teams, and they use equipment that is specialized to carry out their duties, like backboards. On a team of EMTs, one attends to the needs of the patient while another drives to and from the scene of the emergency. In some cases, EMTs work alongside paramedics as part of a Life Flight team, where patients in serious health condition are airlifted to trauma centers.

EMTs are generally part of the team that transfers patients to health facilities, often specifically to emergency rooms. EMTs are required to report actions they have taken and observations they have made to the emergency room's staff.

Once EMTs are through with a given emergency operation, they are required to file some basic reports documenting all the actions they have taken with regards to respective patients' health care. They are also supposed to check the state of their equipment at this juncture and see if any supplies require replenishing. In short, EMTs are responsible for ensuring their equipment is always in good working order and that they have sufficient supplies on hand to deal with any emergency.

EMTs not only liaise with paramedics to transport patients to medical facilities, but they also help transport patients from one medical institution to another when such transfers are required, often involving ambulances used for private services.

Sometimes, though, it is necessary to transfer patients to different medical institutions that are better equipped to handle particular injuries or illness. Some patients being transferred require long-term health care, and so their destination may be a nursing home or similar facility. Although the NREMT certification makes emergency medical technicians marketable, their salaries are often raised to correspond to their experience, among other factors. Some EMTs earn more than $51,000 annually.

This book will explain the material you need to know in order to thoroughly prepare for the NREMT exam. Although a lot of substantive medical information is provided, you also need to read elsewhere extensively, especially when it comes to human anatomy, how various organs function and specific life-saving treatments.

Chapter 3: Nature of Emergencies EMTs Encounter

Sometimes EMTs encounter critical medical emergencies associated with a patient's airway, ventilation or respiration. A person's respiratory system consists of several parts, and each part can affect how successful (or unsuccessful) a treatment is. It is important to conduct a thorough assessment and provide appropriate treatment. Your success in this area will be dependent on your understanding of the respiratory system and what steps need to be taken in case of an emergency. Respiratory emergencies may comprise cardiology, cardiovascular issues and resuscitation. Therefore, you must be thoroughly versed in all human body systems.

EMTs may encounter obstetric and gynecological emergencies which require them to be knowledgeable enough in these areas to provide appropriate treatment.

There are also many trauma-related emergencies that EMTs are called upon to handle.

Given the wide scope of possible emergencies, EMTs require ample knowledge regarding terms commonly used in the medical field, as well as medical procedures of a specialized nature. You can rely on this guide to detail many of the topics you need to study in order to pass your NREMT exam and become a certified EMT.

Information on the EMS

There are several guidelines within Emergency Medical Services (EMS) in terms of appropriate procedures you may perform while providing life-saving care. It is important that you learn what those procedures are and how to implement them.

EMS is a response system that offers care for people who have fallen ill or been injured. This system has different components that include personnel and training as well as equipment, all necessary for providing effective response to emergencies. The EMS system has ambulances, first responders and emergency dispatchers, as well as oversight by medical professionals. In the U.S. there is an act in place containing provisions pertaining to EMTs who have disabilities but who, in some circumstances, are able to provide emergency services.

About EMS Medical Direction

Every system of EMS is guided by protocols written by a physician in charge which provides authority for EMTs to provide health care. These particular protocols comprise the scope of medical practice for the EMTs. However, it should be noted that sometimes some modifications or additional treatments may be directed by medical control. The medical director is in charge of establishing training for EMTs.

Health Services Integrated With Emergency Services

Emergency services provided by EMTs are just a start for patients' medical care. As such, the health care EMTs provide needs to be well integrated with the services offered by the hospitals receiving emergency patients. In fact, a good number of EMS systems now have procedures in place for time-sensitive emergencies such as strokes or heart attacks in order to ensure that hospitals are prepared to treat these critical cases as quickly as possible.

Evaluation of Services Provided by EMTs

EMTs are continually evaluated in order to ensure patients receive the highest quality care. These evaluations involve a review of the care patients are receiving and rate of error reduction. Errors are sometimes based on lack of knowledge or skills. Errors are inevitable, but EMTs are obliged to recognize errors and work towards avoiding and reducing them as much as possible.

Use of Information Systems in Emergency Services

Emergency services now rely a lot on computer technology, and data is gathered and utilized for a wide range of purposes that include staffing, justifying equipment use and identifying training requirements.

System Financing

Every emergency medical system requires funding in order to continue running its operations effectively. Such funding is collected from different sources, sometimes in the form of fees charged to patients, donations, grants provided by various organizations and/or taxes. It is the role of EMTs to accurately document any care given to patients, and also to obtain signatures from patients for purposes of billing.

EMTs' Role in Emergency Prevention

EMS is part of the overall public health-care system, and since one of the system's goals is to reduce health-care costs, EMTs play a crucial role in this due to their extensive knowledge regarding typical injuries and causes of illnesses common in various communities. As such, the wealth of knowledge EMTs have can be utilized when designing preventative measures.

Chapter 4: Anatomy & Pathophysiology

This section discusses potential NREMT questions associated with breathing issues, and so it is important that you are familiar with all the parts of the respiratory system, along with key medical terminology. It is also important that you are skilled enough to apply appropriate medical techniques and know how to use necessary equipment when people are having breathing difficulties.

Anatomy of the Respiratory System

A person's respiratory system is divided into the upper and lower airways. Both sections of this system play a crucial part in facilitating breathing and the exchange of gases.

The upper airway comprises the person's oral cavity, made up of the nose and mouth, tongue and jaw, and larynx and pharynx. The upper airway facilitates the passage of air in and out of a person's lungs when someone is inhaling or exhaling. This section of the airway is also responsible for humidifying and warming the air.

As you prepare for the NREMT exam, it is important that you learn everything possible about the respiratory system and the nasopharynx, as well as the trachea.

A person's lower airway is comprised of the trachea as well as the lungs. The trachea is divided into two segments—the right and left main stem bronchi. It is possible to see how these bronchi have branched to join the right lung and the left, the right lung comprising the upper and middle lobes as well as the lobes on the lower side. Each of those lobes has millions of alveoli, which are small air sacs within which the exchange of gases takes place.

To clearly understand how the lower airway functions, you need to read about the thyroid cartilage and the cricoid cartilage, the cricothyroid membrane and also the alveoli.

Variation Between Airways of a Child and an Adult

Although the anatomy of the airways of a child and an adult is basically the same, there are still noticeable differences. For one, a child generally has smaller airways than an adult, and that applies to both the upper and lower airways. This means a child has a smaller nose, mouth and trachea. Fortunately, these passages also have more flexibility than those of an adult, but the small size means children are more prone to obstructed airways than adults. It might seem an advantage that a child's tongue is smaller in comparison to an adult's, but this organ ends up taking up a disproportionate amount of space.

The Physiology of the Respiratory System

The respiratory system's physiology includes respiration and ventilation, both of these processes being purely involuntary. This means respiration and ventilation happen on reflex, and a person doesn't usually need to think about them. To assist these natural functions, EMTs need to know the distinct difference between ventilation, oxygenation and respiration.

About Ventilation

Ventilation in the medical sense simply means breathing, and it entails the inward inhalation of air and outward exhalation of air into and out of a person's lungs. This process of ventilation requires the use of body structures like the diaphragm as well as the intercostal muscles, which contract in tandem to allow inhalation. These muscles relax as a person exhales. In instances where ventilation is not sufficient, it means there is also inadequate oxygenation. Hence it becomes necessary to assess to what degree assistance may be required in ventilating.

To better understand the concept of ventilation, you need to study the process of inhalation and exhalation, dyspnea and partial pressure.

About Oxygenation

Oxygenation is the process of delivering oxygen into a person's blood cells through the hemoglobin. The tissues and organs of the body require oxygenation in order to function as they should. There are different reasons delivery of oxygen to the body organs could be disrupted, among them altered physiological states, high altitudes and spaces where availability of oxygen is limited like enclosed areas.

It is important to be able to identify situations where a person is experiencing poor oxygenation. Some of the signs include confusion and tachypnea as well as cyanosis. In order to understand this topic better, you need to read further about hypoxia and hypoxic drive, cyanosis as well as tachypnea.

About Respiration

A person's body cells need oxygen. They also need to eliminate carbon dioxide, and respiration is the process of exchanging gases that occurs within the lungs. A person's body receives oxygen by way of inhalation while it eliminates carbon dioxide by way of exhalation. There are also processes of a physiological nature, one of them being diffusion, which allow respiration to take place. It is important to have sufficient ventilation in order for respiration to occur. However, even when the level of ventilation is good, optimal exchange of gases at the cellular level cannot be guaranteed.

To understand the concept of respiration even better, you need to learn more about external and cellular respiration as well as surfactant.

Pathophysiology of Respiration

Respiration is not as simple as it often appears. There are several body systems working closely together to ensure respiration is sufficient, but there is always some danger lurking somewhere with the potential of disrupting that process. Some of the factors with the potential to disrupt the process of respiration will be explained next.

Factors Associated with the Nervous System

The nervous system has an important role to play in the process of respiration. For example, the chemoreceptors within a person's nervous system are in charge of monitoring the spinal fluid's pH, and also the oxygen and carbon dioxide level. On the basis of those two levels, the body's nervous system transmits signals to different respiratory centers within the brain, and that has the effect of altering the rate of respiration or breathing depth. You need to read more on chemoreceptors as you prepare for the NREMT exam.

The Ratio & Mismatch of Ventilation vs. Perfusion

The ratio of ventilation versus perfusion refers to the flow of air entering the lungs as blood also flows into those same lungs. Ideally, those two variables ought to match, yet due to inadequate exchange of gases, there is often a mismatch.

Factors Influencing Pulmonary Ventilation

There are pulmonary related factors which end up affecting the adequacy of ventilation, and these factors can be either intrinsic or extrinsic. Intrinsic factors often comprise responses of an allergic nature, infections of the lungs and blockage of airflow into and out of a person's lungs such as when the tongue blocks the airway. Extrinsic factors include airway blockage caused by interference by a foreign body or trauma that affects either the airway or the chest. To better understand the issue of pulmonary ventilation, it is important that you read about hypercapnia in depth.

Factors Affecting Respiration

Respiration can be affected by both internal and external factors. External factors include altitude or oxygen's partial pressure. Carbon monoxide may affect the efficiency of a person's respiration.

Internal factors mostly have to do with disease as well as conditions known to reduce the surface area of the part of the lung responsible for the exchange of gases. Such diseases include infections, pulmonary edema or chronic obstructive pulmonary disease (COPD). In order to understand how respiration can be interfered with, you need to read up on intrapulmonary shunting.

Conditions that Compromise the Circulatory System

There are some conditions that can affect blood circulation and the efficiency of respiration. Such factors may reduce the oxygenation of tissues. When a person's blood flow is interrupted, it sometimes happens due to a pulmonary embolism, a range of traumatic injuries or tension pneumothorax. At other times, such interruptions happen due to cardiac issues that deter the person's heart from efficiently pumping oxygenated blood, and so not enough of that blood can reach the tissues of the body or other body organs. You need to read about tension pneumothorax and pulmonary embolism in order to be better prepared to answer NREMT questions.

Chapter 5: Assessing a Patient in an Emergency Situation

Among the very first things you must do upon arrival at the scene of an emergency is assess how well a patient is breathing. As you carry out your assessment, there are a number of factors you need to take into account.

Sufficient Breathing vs. Breathing that is Abnormal

One of the factors you need to assess is the patient's rate of respiration, and from your assessment, you should be able to determine if that is high or low enough to be considered abnormal. You should evaluate whether the patient's breathing is labored or not, and how deep the breathing is. It is also important that you assess the level of the patient's consciousness. In order to understand the concept of abnormal breathing, you need to read more on 'breathing work' and breathing that is labored, retractions and ataxic respirations, agonal gasps and apnea, as well as Cheyne-Stokes respiration.

How to Assess Respiration

Even when breathing seems normal, the exchange of gases could still be insufficient. One of the ways oxygenation is assessed within a pre-hospital setting is by use of a pulse oximeter. When conducting a brief assessment of the patient's respiration, also assess the patient's level of consciousness as there is a chance of it being affected if the patient becomes hypoxic or has carbon dioxide levels that are too high.

One of the indicators of an oxygenation problem is the patient's skin color, which will often turn a little bluish. The lips and nails may also be affected. You need to read further on the concepts of pulse oximetry and end-tidal capnography to be in a position to appropriately answer questions related to respiration in the NREMT exam.

How to Keep a Patient's Airway Open

It is important to ensure the patient's airway is open at all times, and you should take exceptional care in instances where the patient is unresponsive. It is common to find the tongue dropping towards the back of the patient's throat during a period of unconsciousness, and this can easily cause obstruction.

An EMT should be able to take the necessary measures to keep a patient's airway open. You need to put the patient in a supine position if that is possible because the position is very effective in maintaining the airway open. There are other ways of opening the airway of an unconscious patient, but you need to do a thorough assessment of the situation and the state of the patient before you decide on a particular technique. Be aware that if you use a method that is inappropriate, you could end up injuring the patient further as opposed to helping.

'Head Tilt-Chin Lift' Technique

Many medics prefer the use of the 'head tilt-chin lift' technique to open the airway of a patient. This is a technique that involves gently lifting the patient's jaw while at the same time pressing the patient's forehead down. This technique puts the affected patient in what is referred to as 'sniffing position,' a preferred position when ventilating the patient manually and also when intubation is required.

The Jaw-Thrust Technique

The 'jaw-thrust' technique serves as an alternative method of opening a patient's airway. It is recommended particularly for patients whose injuries are suspected to affect the spine or neck. This technique entails moving the patient's jaw in an upward direction by putting your fingers right behind the jaw and gently lifting.

The Mouth-Opening Technique

Sometimes you may different techniques like those already described and yet fail to open the patient's mouth. You cannot be at ease when the patient is not able to open the mouth as this is crucial to ventilation. To open the patient's mouth effectively, you can use your thumb and index finger, pushing downwards on the patient's teeth on the lower side of the mouth using the thumb. In the meantime, push the patient's teeth on the upper side of the mouth using your index finger.

The Suctioning Technique

A patient's airway may be obstructed by secretions like mucus, vomit or blood, and for this reason, an EMT should be skilled in suctioning such secretions from a patient's mouth, and sometimes out of a patient's nose. Suctioning is often necessary before intubation because it helps medical staff have a better view of the patient's vocal cords. It is sometimes obvious when a patient is in need of suctioning, like in cases where significant quantities of blood or vomit are visible. In other instances, the need for suctioning becomes obvious when you hear the patient making gurgling sounds.

Use of Equipment

Equipment used for suctioning often includes portable suction devices or mounted suction units, both of which can provide vacuum pressure that helps to remove unwanted secretions. It is advisable to choose your suction catheter on the basis of the patient's needs at the time of the emergency. Two types of catheters are commonly used, one being the rigid-tip type known as 'Yankauer,' and the other a soft-tip one that is flexible and sometimes known as the French catheter. The former is used to suction from the mouth while the latter suctions from the patient's nose or trachea.

Suctioning Techniques

It is important that you ensure you assemble the required equipment before you begin the suctioning process, and that includes the particular suction catheter you have decided is best to use on the patient. The next step involves turning on the device, ensuring you have set it at 300 mmHg. Insert the device tip inside the mouth of the patient as far as you are able to see and not beyond that point. After that, begin suctioning, and as you do, keep withdrawing the catheter out of the patient's mouth.

You are advised to restrict your suctioning period to just 15 seconds when dealing with adult patients and 10 seconds when dealing with children. To be better prepared to answer questions on the issue of suctioning, read further about the Yankauer and French suctioning devices.

About Airway Adjuncts

Airway adjuncts are handy in keeping the airways of patients open by keeping the patient's tongue from becoming a blockage within the airway. Airway adjuncts come in two main types, oropharyngeal and nasopharyngeal. Which airway adjunct you use depends on the patient's level of consciousness, and because identifying the appropriate device to use is critical, you need to do a thorough assessment of your patient first.

The Oropharyngeal Airway Adjunct

This oral device that serves as an oral airway is put inside the patient's mouth with the aim of preventing the patient's tongue from relaxing and ending up becoming a dangerous blockage within the airway. The device is normally used when dealing with patients already breathing on their own, as well as ones requiring manual ventilation. An important thing to note is that the oropharyngeal airway adjunct is recommended only for patients who are unresponsive and have no gag reflex, described as 'intact.'

The Nasopharyngeal Airway Adjunct

A person's nasal airway is another option through which an airway can be maintained. In fact, it is often preferable when dealing with patients with an intact gag reflex.' This device is also good for patients with altered consciousness levels; those not in a position to protect their own airways. You need to read more on the adjunct, oropharyngeal and the nasopharyngeal airways to be better prepared for the relevant NREMT questions.

How to Maintain a Patient's Airway

If you have a patient whose spine is uninjured, you can opt to put them in what is referred to as a 'recovery position' in order to maintain their airway. This position entails rolling the patient's body to one side with the arm on the lower side extended. In the meantime, the patient's upper hand is put under his or her cheek. This is a position known to deter the patient's tongue from creating a blockage within the airway, hence lowering the aspiration risk in case the patient vomits. It will be helpful to read more about the recovery position.

About Supplemental Oxygen

Hypoxia means a part of the body is not receiving sufficient oxygen. Patients who are hypoxic require oxygen supplementation. Some of the symptoms of hypoxia include shortness of breath and confusion, as well as the skin and nail beds turning bluish. You also need to consider using supplemental oxygen when assisting the patient using manual ventilation.

How to Deliver Oxygen

There are various devices used when delivering oxygen for supplemental purposes, one of them being cylinders. Liquid oxygen is also available but is most commonly used by patients at home. Oxygen cylinders are available in varying sizes; the ones EMTs and paramedics commonly take with them for use in the field are referred to as 'D' and 'M.'

Other Field Equipment

Other equipment is often required for oxygen delivery, and this includes pressures regulator. This is equipment that is relied upon to decrease oxygen pressure so that it is released up to a level that is safe, ranging from 40 psi–70 psi.

EMTs may also require a flowmeter, which facilitates flow in specific liters per given duration. Modern regulators often have flowmeters already incorporated, meaning your role is simply to dial in your chosen liter flow.

Required Procedures in Oxygen Administration

Whenever it is time to administer oxygen, you must inspect the oxygen cylinder before proceeding, removing the seal as you do this. It is also your role to crack the cylinder, a move that entails opening the valve and then closing it using the tank key.

It is important that you attach the regulator and flowmeter to the oxygen tank. Once you have identified the delivery device for the oxygen, such as a mask or nasal cannula, attach it to the regular or flowmeter's nipple before turning the flowmeter up to the rate you deem suitable in terms of liters/minute.

Hazards Involved

One thing that should be understood is that oxygen does not burn in a spontaneous manner. Rather, it only supports combustion. As such, EMTs, like everyone else, need to be extra careful about the environments in which they handle oxygen. You should ensure you do not use oxygen in close proximity to a flame or sparks including fireplaces and lit cigarettes.

Don't leave the oxygen cylinder leaning or standing against some wall. Instead, the cylinder should be placed somewhere lying down, except for situations where it has its own specialized cart.

Oxygen can also become toxic, and an EMT ought to take the issue of toxicity into account when giving supplemental oxygen. If oxygen is given in excess, it can harm body tissues, but such fear should not be the basis for depriving a hypoxic person of much-required oxygen. It is important to read more extensively about pressure regulators and flowmeters, as well as oxygen-related toxicity.

Equipment for Oxygen Delivery

Within a pre-hospital environment, where EMTs usually operate, oxygen for supplemental purposes is normally delivered by way of a nasal cannula, bag mask or a non-breather mask. If you use a non-breather mask, you need to set the rate of oxygen flow at 10–15 liters for every minute, so it delivers around 95 percent oxygen. This method is best used when assisting patients who are, though breathing without aid, thought to be hypoxic.

You can also use a nasal cannula while setting the rate of oxygen flow at 1–6 liters for every minute. This is mostly appropriate when assisting patients who are not able to tolerate use of a mask. A nasal cannula has the capacity to deliver around 24–44 percent oxygen.

If you choose the option of an oxygen bag mask, which is welcome when assisting patients who need help with ventilation, you should set the flow of oxygen at 15 liters for every minute. This method can succeed in delivering oxygen to almost 100 percent capacity. To understand this area of delivering supplemental oxygen better, you need to read further on non-breather and partial non-breather, the nasal cannula, venturi mask and the bag mask device.

Ventilation by Artificial Means

Often when patients are being assisted in an emergency situation, it is necessary to provide them with assisted ventilation, particularly when they are unable to breathe sufficiently and/or are described as being apneic. To help in ventilation, EMTs often use a Continuous Positive Airway Pressure (CPAP) machine, a mechanical ventilator or a conventional bag mask. To better understand assisted ventilation, you can read up on passive ventilation, mechanical ventilation and gastric distension.

About CPAPs

EMTs use CPAPs to ensure sufficient air enters the patient's lungs, but this technique is only meant to be used on patients already able to breathe on their own. CPAP is intended to improve tidal volume and oxygenation while reducing the patient's breathing efforts (often described as 'work'). To understand the concept of a CPAP you need to read more on compliance and Bilevel Positive Airway Pressure (BiPAP or BPAP).

Unique Respiratory Methods

Once in a while, EMTs come across emergency situations that require the use of unconventional respiratory techniques, and as long as the EMTs can assist the patient positively until arrival at a medical facility, they are allowed to apply these. Some of these unique methods are detailed next.

Use of Stomas

'Stoma' means an opening that is created in the middle of a patient's neck. This opening is used as a passage for inserting a tracheostomy tube, although there are instances where the stoma is used on its own as an airway, without the tube.

In such instances, the patient's airway on the upper side is bypassed, and there is, therefore, a need to humidify the stoma in order to prevent possible development of mucus plugs. Whenever you are trying to deliver oxygen to someone who has a stoma, it is important to use a tracheostomy mask. However, when ventilation is being performed manually on a patient who already has a tracheostomy tube, you need to ensure a bag mask is attached to that tracheostomy tube for proper ventilation. When the patient being assisted has just a stoma, it's best to use a child's mask, which you should connect to the bag before placing it over the patient's stoma in order to facilitate ventilation. It is advisable that you read more on stoma and tracheostomies in preparation for the NREMT exam.

Airway Obstruction

Sometimes people find themselves with obstructed airways owing to mucus plugs which end up blocking airflow. Other times airflow is blocked because there is swollen tissue along the airway.

However, the most common cause of an obstructed airway is a foreign body that is making it difficult for air to enter and exit the lungs. Foreign bodies many times include food particles, and when it comes to children of a young age, even coins and toy parts are common. Once one of these is lodged within the airway, it becomes pretty difficult to get air into the lungs.

Sometimes you can tell when someone has a blocked airway when they wheeze or produce stridor or weak cough. You can tell a person has a completely obstructed airway if you notice signs of cyanosis, being unable to speak or losing consciousness. To understand this issue of airway obstruction better, you need to read more on both mild and severe airway obstruction, as well as stridor. Stridor is a harsh sound that a person produces, often with vibrations, when the airway is blocked.

Respiration-Related Emergencies

In times of emergency, you may be required to evaluate a patient for respiratory problems and then treat them. As you do this, you need to be aware that your patient's respiratory condition is likely to affect other forms of treatment that you administer. Next, you will learn about some emergencies and the varying conditions in which EMTs find patients.

Carbon Dioxide Retention and Hypoxic Drive

This is one common emergency that is associated with respiration. Sometimes a person retains carbon dioxide in unhealthy levels due to the presence of a lung ailment, the most common culprit being COPD. This condition alters the drive a patient has to breathe, yet in ordinary circumstances, a rise in carbon dioxide levels would lead to the affected person breathing deeper and faster.

When a person has gotten used to living with high carbon dioxide levels in the body, meaning it is a chronic condition, the person's breathing-related drive eventually adjusts so that it corresponds to the low level of oxygen the body is accustomed to. Such an adjusted drive is described as a 'hypoxic' drive.

About Dyspnea

Dyspnea is a situation where a person is short of breath, a development that can be triggered by different causes. A respiratory ailment is one such cause, such as asthma or COPD. Dyspnea can also be caused by pulmonary edema, airway obstruction or anxiety. As an EMT you may suspect a patient has dyspnea if you see symptoms of rapid, shallow breathing or anxiety. When trying to identify the best treatment under the prevailing circumstances, seek to address the actual cause underlying those symptoms.

Infection of the Upper & Lower Airways

Airway infections are brought about by a wide range of causes, one of them being croup. Croup normally affects children. It involves a child's larynx and trachea becoming infected and inflamed.

Other common causes include Respiratory Syncytial Virus (RSV) and pneumonia. Infections affect a person's lower or upper airway, and common symptoms are wheezing, coughing and shortness of breath. The treatment you administer will vary depending on the patient's overall condition and environment, but generally, bronchodilators come in handy, as well as steroids. Supplemental oxygen may also be helpful.

Acute Pulmonary Edema

The term 'pulmonary edema' is used in reference to the presence of excessive fluid in a person's lungs, a development that can emerge all of a sudden owing to congestive heart failure. You can suspect a person has pulmonary edema if you notice a patient coughing while appearing to be short of breath and producing sputum that is frothy and pinkish. Sometimes the person develops breathing 'crackles.' Such patients are typically treated using oxygen as well as Lasix (furosemide).

About COPD

COPD damages a person's alveoli. Often, it develops as a result of smoking. Its common symptoms are coughing, wheezing and shortness of breath. EMTs can treat COPD using bronchodilators, supplemental oxygen or steroids.

About Asthma & Hay Fever

Asthma is a chronic health condition that causes a person to produce more mucus than normal and have inflamed and constricted airways. Common asthma symptoms are wheezing, dyspnea and coughing. EMTs can treat asthma with steroids or bronchodilators.

As for hay fever, a person develops it as a result of reacting to an allergen, and its symptoms are sneezing, a runny nose and sometimes coughing. You need to treat hay fever with decongestants as well as antihistamines.

About Anaphylaxis

Anaphylaxis is a serious allergic reaction. This is a health condition that can end up being life-threatening, as it can cause a person's airway to swell, restricting airflow and subsequently dropping blood pressure to a dangerous level.

Some symptoms of anaphylaxis are hives, difficulty breathing and stridor. You can treat this medical condition with epinephrine or effective airway management.

About Spontaneous Pneumothorax

Pneumothorax occurs when air enters a person's pleural space. This can happen in a spontaneous manner owing to an infection of the lungs, or for reasons that are not readily identifiable.

EMTs can suspect spontaneous pneumothorax if a person has chest pain and other symptoms such as dyspnea or lessened breathing sounds in the affected area. You can treat spontaneous pneumothorax by inserting a tube into the chest in order to eliminate the air that has accumulated in the wrong space.

About Pleural Effusion

Pleural effusion is a medical condition where fluid accumulates right outside a person's lungs and within the pleural space. This condition can be a result of an infection or congestive heart failure, and it could also be caused by cancer. Its symptoms are decreased sounds of breathing in the affected area and shortness of breath.

EMTs cannot effectively treat people with this condition, as this is done by removing the fluid using a hospital-based procedure, but they can make the patient as comfortable as possible by administering oxygen on a supplemental basis, assuming the person appears to be hypoxic.

About Pulmonary Embolism

A pulmonary embolism refers to a situation where there is a blood clot in a person's lung. Such a clot will often have developed elsewhere in the body and moved into the lung due to blood circulation. The clot decreases the level of oxygen in a person's body, and it can be a life-threatening situation.

You can suspect a person has a pulmonary embolism if you see symptoms such as dyspnea and hypoxia, or tachycardia. Once EMTs have transported a patient with a pulmonary embolism to the hospital, it is usual for hospital staff to administer blood thinners.

About Hyperventilation

A person is said to have developed hyperventilation if their rate of respiration is abnormally high. This condition is usually a result of pain and anxiety, although fever is also sometimes the cause. For effective treatment, medical staff must address the cause underlying the symptoms.

About Environmental/Industrial Contaminants

A person can fall ill from inhaling environmental contaminants, some of which may be industrial, and these include chemicals and others substances or gases. Many of these end up irritating the person's airway, a good example being carbon monoxide.

A person affected by such contaminants usually shows symptoms of coughing and dyspnea, although at times the symptoms include an altered consciousness level. EMTs can make use of supplemental oxygen to treat the patient, or they can follow other effective ways of airway management.

About Foreign Body Aspiration

Foreign body aspiration refers to a situation where a person inhales something other than air, for example, food or another object. You can suspect this condition if you observe symptoms of stridor or shortness of breath.

EMTs can treat such a condition by way of airway management and other appropriate care. Once a patient has been transported to the hospital, medical staff will remove the obstructing foreign body.

About Tracheostomy Dysfunction

Patients with a tracheostomy tube sometimes develop different complications, some of which could be blockage of their airway by mucus plugs, bleeding or a dislodged tube. An EMT can suspect tracheostomy dysfunction in a patient if a person presents with hypoxia, cyanosis or a blocked airway.

To treat this condition, it is important to, first of all, assess its severity. For instance, if the airway has been obstructed by a mucus plug, the EMT can simply suction the tracheostomy tube then change the cannula on the inner side.

About Cystic Fibrosis

Cystic fibrosis is a chronic, inherited disease which affects a person's digestive system as well as the lungs. You can suspect cystic fibrosis if the patient shows symptoms of wheezing, extraordinarily high production of mucus and dyspnea. This condition can be treated away from the hospital by suctioning and provision of supplemental oxygen, or by administering medication to loosen the mucus.

In order to understand these concepts better, you need to read more on chronic obstructive pulmonary disease, allergens and bronchiolitis, epiglottitis and bronchodilators, emphysema and status asthmaticus.

Additional Emergency Respiratory Care

It may be necessary to administer additional treatment besides those already explained, but you need to ensure you completely understand any procedures that you undertake as well as the use of various emergency equipment associated with respiration.

The Metered-Dose Inhaler

The metered-dose inhaler is a tiny spray canister that you can use in delivering medications to a person's lungs to help in respiration. Examples of treatments that are conveniently administered through a metered dose-inhaler are steroids, meant to reduce inflammation, and bronchodilators, meant to open a person's airways.

The Small-Volume Nebulizer

The small-volume nebulizer efficiently delivers medication meant to help improve respiration by having the patient inhale a fine mist. One of the most common medications delivered through small-volume nebulizers is albuterol. This medication serves as a bronchodilator and is used in treating medical conditions like asthma or COPD.

Chapter 6: Cardiology & Resuscitation

There are many emergencies that arise involving the heart, and as an EMT it is important that you are aware of the actions necessary to take within the few minutes that may be available to save a person's life. This section of the book will guide you through what you need to know to correctly answer NREMT questions on cardiology and resuscitation. After reading this guide, follow up by studying other textbooks about health issues related to cardiology.

Cardiac Anatomy & Physiology

A person's cardiovascular functions are accomplished by a system comprising arteries and veins as well as capillaries, plus the heart itself. As an EMT you will need to be well versed with the entire system and how it functions, and this means you should also know its potential for poor functioning and ailments. This knowledge is of fundamental importance if you are to excel at managing associated emergencies.

The Function of the Heart

The cardiovascular system's basic function is ensuring oxygenated blood flows throughout a person's body. The system relies on the atrium, aorta and ventricles to ensure such distribution is precise. A person's veins transport blood into the heart while the arteries transport blood from it.

As blood is delivered, byproducts are transported to appropriate body systems for elimination (i.e., the digestive system). For you to understand this concept better you need to read more on the atrium and the ventricles; the aorta; different sections of a person's heart; the heart's major function and in particular its upper and lower chambers; the pathway by which blood flows; autonomic and automaticity and also the sympathetic and parasympathetic nervous system.

Blood Circulation

Blood circulation refers to how blood flows from a person's heart to body tissues and other parts of the body before returning to the heart. In order to have a well-functioning blood circulation system, a person needs to have sufficient blood volume and patent valves, as well as vessels that are functional and which facilitate smooth blood flow.

In order to be well prepared to answer NREMT questions on this area of blood circulation, you need to read further on myocardium and stroke volume; coronary arteries and the aortic valve; dilation and automaticity; the sympathetic and parasympathetic nervous system and cardiac output.

Regarding Cardiac Pathophysiology

According to the Center for Disease Control (CDC) in the U.S., one out of four Americans has some form of heart disease. The most prevalent heart illnesses will be explained next.

Atherosclerosis

Atherosclerosis involves plaque building up against the blood vessels' inner walls, causing an obstruction in the blood flow as well as contracted and dilated vessels.

To enable you to feel confident about answering the relevant NREMT exam questions correctly, you need to read in more detail about ischemia and cardiac arrest, acute lumen and myocardial infarction, occlusion and thromboembolism.

Acute Coronary Syndrome

Acute coronary syndrome can be described as a conglomeration comprising symptoms that arise as a result of myocardial ischemia. This syndrome falls into two different categories that we will describe next.

Angina Pectoris

Angina pectoris is a heart disease that, while sometimes painful, is not considered life-threatening. The reason a person feels pain due to angina pectoris is that there is reduced flow of oxygen, also referred to as an arterial spasm. Often the affected person feels pain when undergoing stress or exertion of a physical nature. The pain is located in the middle of the chest, and patients describe the experience as squeezing or a sensation of pressure similar to what a person feels when experiencing acid reflux (GERD).

Sometimes a patient with angina pectoris might experience pain in the jaw or arm, and sometimes in both those places, and they may also be nauseated. Angina does not lead to the death of any heart cells. Nevertheless, there is a chance of it causing arrhythmias, in which case the condition serves as a warning to take preventative measures before a more serious heart disease can develop.

Acute Myocardial Infarction

Acute myocardial infarction (AMI) involves sweating and pressure within the chest, serious nausea and a feeling of squeezing in the arm or jaw, the lower part of the back, and sometimes, abdominal pain.

There are also patients who manifest varying symptoms from those described, while others do not show any symptoms whatsoever as the illness sets in. Those who experience pain have a blockage in their artery, a development that has the potential to cause serious irreversible damage. In fact, AMI can lead to sudden death. In order to understand these concepts with more clarity and be ready to tackle NREMT questions, it is advisable to read more on the signs and symptoms associated with acute coronary syndrome (ACS); the symptom differential that exists between gender categories and age demographics; differences existing between angina pectoris and AMI; and nitroglycerin regime and syncope.

Cardiogenic Shock

Low cardiac output ends up reducing oxygenation within the body just as it causes the heart to function poorly. This inefficiency of the heart contributes greatly to a failure to deliver oxygenated blood to the rest of the blood. If this situation persists, the affected person might sustain organ damage. To understand this concept better, you need to read more on signs and symptoms associated with cardiogenic shock, as well as the period it takes for a patient to suffer cardiogenic shock following AMI.

Congestive Heart Failure

Congestive heart failure is a heart disease whereby the mechanism through which blood is pumped by the heart becomes weaker than normal, resulting in much slower blood distribution. Owing to that poor rate of blood flow, fluid stasis might develop all around the affected person's heart, and the lungs might also become congested. To understand these concepts better, you need to read more about the roles played by the heart's left ventricle as well as its atria, pulmonary edema and dependent edema.

Hypertensive Emergencies

Hypertension is high blood pressure that is not only acute but also chronic, and that goes beyond the normal range. To be able to treat this medical condition effectively, it is important to first identify its common signs and symptoms.

Going by the standpoint of the American Heart Association (AHA), 120/80 is the ideal blood pressure level. The AHA considers 140/90 and anything above that to be high blood pressure and EMTs are expected to be familiar with these standards. They also ought to familiarize themselves with the most common emergencies related to high blood pressure, namely aortic aneurysm, dissecting aortic aneurysm and acute myocardial infarction.

To be able to answer blood-pressure-related question in the NREMT exam, EMTs are advised to read further on the cardiac process involving systolic and diastolic measurements or readings; the ranges considered normal for blood pressure; signs and symptoms associated with emergencies linked to hypertension; and differentiation of the different hypertension-related emergencies.

How to Assess a Patient in Cardiac-Related Emergencies

Assessing a patient in a cardiac emergency is vital irrespective of the environment the patient is in. It is important to get things right during an assessment, including blood pressure level, treatment timing and medication administered.

Assessing the Scene

You need to learn as much as you can about how the incident began, starting with the call to 911 or other emergency number. You also need to observe the particular environment within which you find the patient and encourage the patient to give you as much information as possible. If you can get information pertaining to the incident from eye witnesses, so much the better.

One of the first things you need to address is the patient's stability and safety, using universally accepted precautions. EMTs and other medical personnel are cautioned against assuming anything or allowing themselves to be pigeon-holed by the information they initially gather.

In short, you should not restrict your thinking when it comes to understanding the patient's situation, but use your assessment of the scene to learn about the environment, when the incident began or took place, the pattern of the incident and the duration of the patient's symptoms. It is advisable that you read further about how to assess an emergency scene, especially in relation to cardiac issues.

Important Primary Assessment

As you observe the patient immediately upon arrival, you need to ensure you assess for 'Airway Breathing Circulation' (ABC) in order to determine if you must administer basic cardiopulmonary resuscitation (CPR). Remember, based on the symptoms the patient manifests and the status of the patient, timing is critical.

As an EMT you need to have an automated external defibrillator (AED) on hand as well as supplemental oxygen, and also some backup in the form of Advanced Life Support (ALS) whenever possible. You need to read further on AED and the process of CPR.

About History-Taking

The very first thing EMTs need to address is all the factors that are considered life-threatening. The next step involves taking the patient's history; some of the relevant information is likely to have been gathered at the time of assessing the scene.

It is crucial that you remain calm as you speak to the concerned patient and any witnesses. Speak clearly and concisely. You should take the opportunity to get clarifications on important issues you might have picked up on, and fill in pertinent medical details about the patient and his or her history. You also need to get specific details linked to the present incident and crucial conditions that can be considered comorbid, even as you record the patient's history with similar incidents.

To prepare adequately for the NREMT exam, you need to read more on symptoms linked to respiratory issues, the mnemonic used in assessing the pain a patient is in (OPQRST) and the most crucial questions you need to ask a patient who is alert during an emergency of a cardiac nature.

Patient's Secondary Assessment

A secondary patient assessment is based on the information gathered in the primary assessment. In short, while the primary assessment serves as the foundation in helping the patient, the secondary assessment is more hands-on and specific.

During the secondary assessment, your focus should be on symptoms that are significant and still active, and which will guide further assessment of the patient's respiratory, circulatory and cardiovascular symptoms.

It is important to assess the condition of the patient's skin, including its color and temperature, its turgor and refill of capillaries and so on. It is also important to assess blood pressure and respiration, saturation of oxygen and pulse and the level of pain the patient may be in.

You need to make a point of auscultating the patient's lungs as well as the heart while paying close attention to any major signs or symptoms that might point to complications of a cardiovascular and respiratory nature. In preparation to answer NREMT questions correctly, it is advisable to read further on the procedure used in making observations on a patient's heart as well as lungs, and in assessing those organs.

Chapter 7: Reassessing the Patient

The moment to reassess the patient is when you are organizing for the patient's transportation as well as communicating with the hospital's emergency department. Your reassessment should be along the same lines as your primary assessment, focusing on how the patient is, while also paying attention to changes you may have noticed since carrying out your primary assessment. All the while you should note any complaints by the patient and any additional concerns.

Your focus should also be on any improvements you may have noted since giving the patient emergency treatment, and if the patient has not improved, you should note that as well. You also need to make sure you have accurately completed the necessary documentation, and that you have included any interventions given and their timing. For the sake of performing well in the NREMT exam, you need to read further on how to determine the right frequency to assess a patient's vital signs.

Chest Discomfort and Pain

Whenever a person is experiencing pain or discomfort in the chest, it is considered an important sign that needs to be assessed further and immediate action may need to be taken. Still, it should be noted that not every pain felt in the chest has links to cardiac problems. Nevertheless, it is crucial that assessment is done in a timely manner so that in case a cardiac problem is imminent, it can be swiftly arrested.

Basics of Treating Chest Pain

Fundamental treatment of chest pain includes ensuring the patient is well positioned and measures are taken to ensure his or her basic comfort; appropriate adjustment of the patient's clothing, or removal of some of them and provision of oxygen support using suitable equipment. To be better prepared to answer the NREMT exam questions, it is advisable to read about oxygen titration and mechanisms for delivering oxygen, as well as use of acetylsalicylic acid (ASA or aspirin) and its suitable doses.

Use of Nitroglycerin

Some patients have a high risk of cardiovascular problems especially those who have already experienced related episodes and are relying on nitroglycerin prescriptions. The highest dosage and frequency required for administration of nitroglycerin to alleviate chest pain is three doses per every period of five minutes. You need to take note of some important points relating to administration of nitroglycerin, one of them being the nitroglycerin's expiration date and/or possible contamination, its potency and prescription, as well as pills or patches.

In preparation for the NREMT exam, you need to read further on the dosage of nitroglycerin, the medication's indications as well as contraindications, the necessary steps to take and also precautions as you administer and handle nitroglycerin.

Monitoring of Cardiac Conditions

Often, monitoring of patients' cardiac conditions when away from medical institutions is done using an electrocardiogram (ECG) machine. As an EMT you need to establish if you are within your rightful jurisdiction, in relation to the scope of your practice, as you place electrodes and leads to monitor cardiac conditions.

Before you use the electrodes and leads, it will be necessary for you to assess the patient's skin and prepare it so the electrodes can adhere. Placing such elements calls for accuracy, for the sake of ensuring the ECG is not interfered with by extraneous factors. You need to read further on ECF artifacts, electrode placement and 12-lead ECGs.

Heart Surgery Patients and Cardiac Assistive Devices

It is important to learn how to assist patients who have had heart surgery, as well as those who rely on cardiac assistive devices. There are currently several advanced treatments, and they include surgeries as well as devices of a technological nature that help patients with various heart conditions. It is important that EMTs learn about them to the level where they can be of assistance when handling patients with such devices.

ICD or Implantable Cardiac Defibrillator

The device referred to as an ICD is normally inserted into a patient by a qualified physician either in the chest or the patient's abdomen. This device is useful to patients who are considered to be high risk for arrhythmias, those that could potentially lead to sudden cardiac arrest. The ICD shocks the heart directly in instances when life-threatening arrhythmias occur. In order to comprehend this concept better, you need to read further on the cardiac electrical system and how best to deal with a patient who has an ICD.

Defibrillator Vest

A defibrillator vest is a form of vest with a defibrillator and monitor, as well as voice systems, worn on the outside of a patient's inner clothing. Its role is to deliver high-energy shocks that are similar to those released by AEDs. You need to read more on the precautions required with regards to a patient using a defibrillator vest.

The Left Ventricular Assist Device

Often, patients requiring the use of a left ventricular assist device (LVAD) also require additional assistance in pumping blood. Sometimes the device is set to operate intermittently, pulsing just as a normal heart does. Other times the device is set to pump blood on a continual basis, in which case the person's capacity to palpate pulses is interfered with. It is advisable to read about the difference existing between pulsatile and LVFT (Left Ventricular Filling Time) that is continuous.

Automated External Defibrillator

An automated external defibrillator, or AED, is a device that is semi-automated, and it is also computerized and interactive. It is a device that has helped save the lives of many people who have cardiac emergencies, working to monitor electrical impulses emanating from within a person's heart and delivering necessary shocks via electrodes; all this on the basis of particular arrhythmias that are, in many instances, fatal. AEDs are among the easiest devices to use, and as such, they can effectively be used even by people who are not in the medical profession to help someone in an emergency of cardiac nature. It is advisable to read about the five links associated with the survival chain.

Best Time to Utilize a Defibrillator

Generally, you need to use a defibrillator whenever the person you are trying to assist is non-responsive, has no palpable pulse and the symptoms point to a cardiac emergency. The defibrillator monitors and analyzes the condition to determine if it is necessary to give the patient a shock. Carefully follow the defibrillation's instructions so that you deliver a shock only when it is appropriate. It is important to read more on the functions of an AED in general and the advantages of the device when it is crucial to not to use a defibrillator, bradycardia and also tachycardia.

Use of a Defibrillator & Resuscitation

Different organizations offer lay people CPR training. This is beneficial to everyone as it contributes greatly to positive outcomes in times of emergency. EMTs sometimes come across patients who have already begun receiving CPR, and in such instances, an EMT should take up the role from the layman and continue giving the patient CPR right there on-site. If the person fails to respond to the CPR session and remains unresponsive, then the EMT needs to use an AED. You need to read more on AEDs, CPR and asystole.

Maintaining a Defibrillator

Emergency teams must maintain their AED device. Maintenance includes preventive measures (PM) and periodic quality checks. At the same time, EMTs should learn from the machine's handbook how to operate the device and maintain the equipment properly. It is advisable to read further about means of ensuring an AED functions well, the risks of a legal nature associated with AED use and when to contact the manufacturer when an AED proves non-functional.

Medical Supervision

Some studies pertaining to improvements necessary to enhance the quality of cardiac-related services have emphasized the need for early intervention. It has been found that medical supervision is a crucial inclusion to the protocols, procedures and guidelines associated with the use of AEDs. In an ideal situation, every time an AED has been used, the emergency team ought to undergo a debriefing detailing of the entire emergency situation.

In that session the team would discuss whatever went positively and whatever requires improvement for the sake of future encounters. For the sake of proper preparation for the NREMT exam, you need to read further on the medical director's role when it comes to use of AEDs, and also on goals for quality enhancement in relation to AED use.

Use of Defibrillator on Children

You can safely use an AED or manual defibrillator on children, but it is important to weigh your options as far as device type is concerned, as well as the pads plus infants' pediatric attenuators. You also need to consider what is appropriate for children below eight years old and those above that age. It is advisable to read the recommendations given by the AHA with regard to AED use on children. You will enhance your knowledge by reading about manual defibrillators and options available when there is no pediatric defibrillator available, as well as on pediatric dose attenuators.

Extraordinary Situations

There are some extraordinary situations that fall beyond the scope of what can be termed 'normal' defibrillation situations, and you will see three of such situations discussed next, especially as regards patient safety.

Implanted Pacemakers & Defibrillators

Patients who have heart issues of a chronic nature may have internal devices or devices that are implanted, and it is important to avoid fixing an AED pad directly above such devices. In case you have a situation where the device has been fitted where an AED pad is ordinarily placed, you need to choose a different location for the AED pad, immediately below that device. The two pad positions, anterior and posterior, can be used as well.

Patients who are Wet

As mentioned earlier, it is important to assess the environment immediately upon arriving at the emergency scene. In case the environment is wet or damp, including the location where the patient is, it's unsafe to use an AED considering water is a great conductor of electricity. In short, you should avoid using AEDs under wet circumstances for the safety of both the patient and the team responding to the emergency.

Transdermal Patches

Patients have varying reasons for having medication patches, and it is a good habit to use a glove whenever you remove a patch that has the potential to interfere with placement of an AED or a lead. You need to clean the area properly and dry it so that it has no remaining gel or residue prior to the application of the AED. It is advisable for you to read more on existing alternatives to placement of an AED pad.

About a Child Experiencing Chest Pain

A child may experience chest pain, but usually it is not related to an acute ailment. Such pain is normally considered a condition that is benign and self-limiting. Cardiac incidents involving children usually stem from issues of respiration such as choking, and they occur without the child necessarily having a history of a cardiac problem. To understand this issue better, it is advisable to read about the congenital problems.

Cardiocare & Range of Ages

While it is crucial that emergency care is provided to all patients with concerns of a cardiac nature, it is still important to follow established procedures. Nevertheless, there is sometimes a need to modify these procedures a little bit to correspond to a patient's age and unique medical needs. For example, you could have a child patient who has a history of congenital cardiac problems. The child's heart defects in such a case would call for a different approach from the conventional approach meant for pediatrics.

Similarly, cardiocare involving elderly patients who have had cardiac issues of a chronic nature or cardiovascular disease may require an approach that is somewhat different from that used on a patient who has clear arteries. It is advisable to read more on complications prevalent among elderly patients in order to be well prepared for the NREMT exam.

Care in Instances of Cardiac Arrest

Reports from the AHA indicate that in the U.S. alone there are over 350,000 emergencies associated with cardiac arrest handled away from hospitals every year.

Cardiac arrest is defined as an instance where the heart's electrical system ceases to function, which is different from having a heart attack. In the latter case, blood is prevented from flowing into the heart by a blockage.

How to Prepare to Handle a Cardiac Emergency

It is important that response to a cardiac emergency be both fast and safe. To begin care, assign specific roles to individual members of your EMT team, ensuring there is someone to assess the scene and the environment as well as the method of injury (MOI). It is also important that you check for any other injuries, or potential injuries while taking note of any environmental elements that might have a bearing on the safety of the patient, the team, or the team's ability to give care. In order to better prepare for the NREMT exam, you need to read more about heart attacks and cardiac arrest.

About Defibrillation

Whenever defibrillation is carried out, it is done in league with the people carrying out CPR. They work closely such that they are able to relieve one another in rotation. This ensures there is no single person becoming too exhausted to provide emergency help. EMTs are expected to make use of AEDs at their earliest convenience, and one advantage is that an AED provides the appropriate direction in giving shocks as emergency treatment. Following every defibrillation, the team continues giving CPR to the patient, but what they start off with are compressions. It is advisable to read more about CPR as well as defibrillation and the steps you need to take when making use of AEDs and Return of Spontaneous Circulation (ROSC).

Following Defibrillation

Following defibrillation, the care the patient receives is categorized in three parts, one of them being the patient regaining pulse, the patient failing to regain pulse in which case the AED's recommendation is to provide shock and the patient failing to regain pulse yet without a recommendation from the AED to provide a shock. It is important that you be aware of the jurisdiction policies affecting you as far as procedures within respective scenarios. Read more on scenarios where a patient does not have a pulse and where AED shock is not recommended in order to be well prepared to answer the relevant NREMT questions.

Possible Cardiac Arrest at Transportation Time

It is crucial that a patient be monitored very closely when being transported to a medical facility, and in the event it is noted the patient has ceased to have any palpable pulse, emergency care needs to resume immediately. This applies to instances when a patient who was conscious earlier on suddenly becomes unconscious, and ALS guidelines should be adhered to. You need to read more on the resumption of CPR or initiating it when the patient is in transit to the hospital.

Role Accomplished Through ALS

The ALS team plays a very important role in saving lives in communities. You need to make sure you keep communication channels open and communicate clearly and concisely so as to reap the best benefits from their patient-support services. In case the ALS team is not on hand to help, as an EMT you need to be the patient's most important advocate, recommending only what is best for that patient. The first such recommendation and action would be assisting the patient using the AED as soon as possible.

It is important to remember that for a patient in ventricular fibrillation, timing is crucial, and so the AED directions should be followed to the letter. It is best that you read more on the scope of practice allowed to EMT and ALS teams.

About ROSC

Whenever ROSC is noted in a patient whose pulse was not palpable, this is considered a positive indication. It generally means the patient in question has normal blood following an incident of cardiac arrest. You need to read more on the concept of ROSC.

About Resuscitation

The issue of resuscitation falls under the concept of providing BLS, where it is recognized that it is important to provide high quality care to a person who requires CPR just as much as other individuals requiring assistance for various cardiovascular conditions that are life-threatening. There are established practices to be followed in emergencies requiring BLS, and they are not only standard but also scientific. EMTs need to know them, the actions they need to take and their set sequence.

Factors Influencing BLS

The techniques incorporated in BLS are intended to sustain the life of individuals in emergency situations that are associated with respiration and general airway issues as well as cardiac arrest.

The very basic treatment given to address issues of obstruction of the airway include compressions of the chest as well as assisted breathing, and they are the same basic ones that are intended to improve respiratory function in times of respiratory arrest and blood circulation in times of cardiac arrest or bleeding.

It is important to note that the guidelines for CPR, according to the AHA, have changed. In place of 'airway, breathing and chest compressions' (ABC), 'chest compressions, airway and breathing' (CAB) is now the guide. The reason for this change, introduced in 2010, is that there is sufficient data to confirm that patients who receive chest compressions without delay have better medical outcomes. This means it is best to do chest compressions as the first step in the life-saving emergency process.

Aspects of ALS actually make enhancements on the gains of BLS, and their major differences are with regard to patient monitoring and administration of IV fluids as well as medication.

How to Determine if BLS is Necessary

In order to objectively tell if a person in an emergency situation requires BLS, which is inclusive of CPR, you need to establish if the patient is able to breathe independently and whether you observe patency of the airway. You also need to make certain circulation is sufficient, something you can confirm by way of checking pulse palpation and also ensuring there is no indication of possible bleeding. It is advisable that you read more on the fundamentals of ABC and CAB as well as CPR.

About CPR

CPR is carried out in order to help a person presenting with neither pulse nor respiration. The technique became acceptable during the 1960s, and it has since evolved as a fundamental method of assisting people in a crisis involving cardiovascular and respiratory problems. It is a technique effectively taught to health-care personnel as well as lay people.

The major goal of giving a person CPR is to help the person regain spontaneous breathing function, as well as normal circulation of blood following stoppage of both these functions. To carry out CPR effectively, it is necessary to perform some maneuvers in an artificial way that people are normally trained in. It is important that you are clear on the main goal of CPR before you sit the NREMT exam.

Steps to Take During CPR

CPR is carried out in five main steps, and they comprise co-operation, collaboration and also communication with the teams concerned with BLS and ALS as well as the ER team. You need to learn more about these critical steps and also the survival chain.

Guidelines for CPR

CPR on its own cannot be considered sufficient treatment for someone in an emergency situation who is not responsive. In fact, you need to assess the person's airway as well as the pulse before beginning CPR. You also should not carry out any compressions on someone who is not responsive even if that person has a pulse. Another thing you should not do is try to give artificial ventilation to someone whose airway is already open and has sufficient respirations.

When CPR Should Not be Started

Sometimes it is not advisable to perform CPR even when it appears like the person needs it, and an EMT should be aware of those scenarios. For starters, you should refrain from giving CPR if you notice the person has a pulse yet is not able to breathe. In such a case, you should help the person by giving alternative respiratory aid. There are also orders that should be followed, specifically 'Do Not Resuscitate' (DNR). Also, if a person shows no sign at all of being alive, EMTs or other personnel should not perform CPR. It is important that you read further on injuries that cannot be survived, rigor and livor mortis and instances when CPR should not be given.

The Moment to End CPR

Normally you initiate CPR with the intention of continuing it until more advanced medical help arrives or until the person you are trying to help is no longer alive. The standards you should adhere to in deciding when to cease CPR can be represented in the mnemonic, STOP, where S stands for Starts breathing, T stands for Transfer of care, O stands for Out of Strength and P stands for Physician's order. You need to remember and learn more about the mnemonic, STOP.

When to Interrupt CPR

The process of CPR is meant to act as an intervention to save a life, and once it has begun, there should be minimal interruption. Many times CPR becomes crucial when there is no ALS on-site, and during transportation of the patient, CPR is still necessary. It is expected that the team present to handle the emergency will perform CPR on a continuous basis, only taking brief necessary breaks, probably to enable the patient to be lifted for transportation and such. When it comes to chest compressions, each interruption should not last over 10 seconds. It is important that you read more on the chest compression fraction.

Chapter 8: Patient Care During an Emergency

The care meant for a patient during an emergency includes more than the technical moves the team performs or the use of medical equipment. In such situations there are several factors that come into play, including the issues that preceded the unfortunate event. You also need to consider whether the environment is safe, if the patient has sustained other not-so-obvious injuries and if the patient has any family members or friends. It is also important to try and establish if there are any witnesses to the incident that caused an emergency situation and to gather what they know. After learning these things, you will be better placed to help create a suitable care plan for the patient.

Positioning the Patient

The appropriate position to put a patient in an emergency situation is on a surface that is flat and firm, and in a position described as 'supine.' This way you can carry out your assessment of the patient better and proceed to give CPR. Whenever possible, it's important to ensure there is adequate space to accommodate two people from the rescuing team as well as equipment necessary to aid the patient, and this should be addressed before emergency procedures begin.

You need to make use of the recovery position when the patient has not sustained any injuries of the spine and is able to breathe independently. For the sake of tackling the relevant NREMT questions with confidence, it is advisable that you read further on the recovery position, supine and logroll, as well as prone.

Assessing Breathing and Patient's Pulse

Prior to starting the process of CPR, it is important to check if the patient who seems to be unresponsive is breathing and has a pulse. You can accomplish this by trying to arouse that patient and observing for 10 seconds. It is important that you read further on the concepts of assessing an unresponsive patient for breathing as well as pulse, means of palpating carotid pulse and also the location of the carotid artery.

Chest Compressions

It is crucial to initiate chest compressions whenever you want to provide high quality CPR to a patient who has no pulse. This involves using a suitable technique, which includes positioning the hands correctly and compressing up to the correct depth. These factors will depend on the patient's age.

When dealing with an adult patient, kneel immediately next to that patient and lace your fingers together with one above the another. Place your laced fingers on the tip of your patient's breastbone and then give compressions at a speed of 100 compressions per minute while keeping the depth a minimum of two inches.

The patient should receive two breaths after every 30 compressions, irrespective of the number of rescuers involved. To learn more about these concepts, you need to read further about how best to position your hands and your arms as you carry out compressions, and also about the appropriate depth you should target when giving compressions to an adult patient.

How to Give CPR to Children or Infants

It is not usual for pediatric patients to suffer cardiac arrest, and when it happens, it is usually in cases where the patient has a history or a pre-existing respiratory issue that ends up causing cardiopulmonary problems. In case you must initiate CPR on a child or an infant, you should aim at giving the appropriate breaths and place your hands appropriately.

If the affected child is from one year old to puberty, place your hand, or both of your hands, on the lower half of the patient's breastbone. How you accomplish that will depend on the size of the child and your hand. As for the depth of the compressions that you give, they should be a minimum of two inches, and the compressions themselves ought to be delivered at 100 per minute. In case only one rescuer is involved in giving the compressions, the ratio of compression-ventilation should be 30:2. However, in case you are working with another rescuer, that rate needs to change and become 15:2.

Children who are one year old or below need to receive compressions at the same rate as others, 100 per minute, but there should be a change in the depth of those compressions. They should be given at a depth of one and a half inches. Also, the placement of your hand and the ratio of CPR should vary depending on the number of rescuers involved. In case only a single rescuer is available, that one should remain by the patient's side while making use of two fingers in compressing the chest immediately below the nipple line of the young patient.

When dealing with an infant and just one rescuer, the ratio of compression to ventilation when providing CPR should be 30:2. In the same circumstances but with two rescuers, one of them should be positioned at the patient's head while the other one should remain at the young patient's feet. Also, the person giving compressions ought to make use of two hands in a manner that they encircle the patient's chest while delivering compressions at the rate of 15:2. It is important that you read further on infant and child compression depth, ischemia and hypoxia and standard position.

Opening Children's Airways

Sometimes children get their upper air passage obstructed, especially because when they are little they like putting objects that are not edible inside their tiny mouths. Such objects sometimes lodge within the air passage causing obstruction, and sometimes even chunks of food do the same after being chewed poorly.

You need to use the same maneuvers whenever you want to help people of different ages open their airways. For example, as discussed earlier, there is a maneuver referred to as 'head tilt-chin lift' that is suitable for patients who do not face a risk of injuring their spine. In instances where risk of injuring the spine is suspected, the suitable maneuver to use is the one referred to as 'jaw thrust' since it poses minimal risk of injuring the spine. You need to read further on maneuvers of opening the airway.

About Airway Obstruction by Foreign Object

For CPR to be carried out there needs to be either an obstruction of the airway, breathing difficulty or both. Sometimes a person's airway is obstructed by a foreign body that is either aspirated or has been stuck after failing to pass smoothly through the air passage. It is important that you assess the patient to see if there is any obstruction, even being caused by the patient's tongue. Use maneuvers that have been recommended in a bid to open the patient's airway.

Recognizing the Presence of a Foreign Body

In case there is a foreign object within the air passage, the patient's body has a way of responding, which includes coughing or gagging. In case that obstructing object is sizeable enough to lead to full obstruction, you may hear the patient produce high-pitched gasping or wheezing, although in some cases the patient may fail to produce any sound whatsoever.

A person who is choking may be able to show that danger by using the universally acknowledged sign, which is placing one hand or both around the neck. Such a person may also exhibit a bluish color on the lips or skin.

Techniques of Opening Airways

There are a number of techniques recommended in trying to help open the airways for people with obstruction, and these are explained next.

The Abdominal Thrust

The Heimlich Maneuver is actually considered the gold standard when it comes to removing foreign objects from a person's airway. When utilizing this technique, the person conducting the rescuing needs to stand right behind the person being assisted, while encircling both the arms around the patient's abdomen.

The person in charge of doing the rescuing forms a fist while placing the fist under the rib cage as well above the patient's navel. In the meantime, the rescuer uses one hand to grasp the fist to get support, and then there is a fast upward thrust. That maneuver ought to go on till the obstructing object is ejected, or until the person with a problem falls unconscious. Thereafter you should carry out an assessment to determine if CPR is necessary.

Chest Thrust

EMTs use the chest thrust when it is not appropriate to use the abdominal thrust. Such cases include when the patient is morbidly obese if the patient happens is lying down or in the case of a pregnant woman. In cases like these, place your fist high on the person's body, on the middle part of the sternum, but not on the lower section. When the person being rescued is in a lying position, kneel beside that patient and employ the heel of your hand in the delivery of thrusts in an upward direction at the sternum's midsection.

Removing Of Foreign Objects from Adults

When trying to get rid of a foreign body obstructing the airway of an adult, employ the thrust maneuver targeting the abdomen. In case that patient is not responsive, you should use the chest thrust maneuver only after observing the patient and manually removing any object that is visible. Where a pregnant woman is concerned, make use of chest thrusts and not abdominal thrusts.

Removing Foreign Objects from Children

In order to remove foreign bodies from a one-year-old child's airway when the child is responsive, use the abdominal thrust maneuver. For a child who is not responsive, it is recommended that you use the chest thrust. You need to observe the patient to see if he or she has a visible object in the airway so that you can remove it before you take action.

Removing Foreign Objects from Infants

Considering the organs of infants are fragile, you should not use abdominal thrusts on infants or children whose age is below a year. Instead, you should use the 'back slap chest thrust' if the patient is responsive. In case the young patient is unresponsive, assess the mouth for any visible object in the airway and remove it if possible.

All in all, you should adhere to the recommendations for infant and child CPR. It is advisable that you read further on recognition of signs of air passage obstruction, stridor and abdominal thrusts, chest thrusts and the back slap maneuver.

About Artificial Ventilation

There are different devices available to help give artificial ventilation, some with oxygen and others without. Make use of the one-way valve pocket mask to ventilate patients via the mouth or stoma. Otherwise, you can use a bag-valve-mask as your standard equipment. To be well prepared for the NREMT exam, you need to read further on stoma as well as gastric ventilation, ventilation and hyperventilation and gastric distention.

Techniques & Devices Involving Circulation

From the very beginning, CPR has always comprised manual chest compressions as well as ventilation, all following different best practices. Today, there is a search for devices that can take over the manual work of CPR, including those which help with compressions and enhancement of circulation. There is a likelihood that new devices, once introduced, could have some impact on compressions' quality for the better, considering quality is currently likely to be compromised once the EMTs or other personnel giving CPR become exhausted.

Working under Unique Circumstances

Dealing with a Pregnant Woman

Some circumstances EMTs work under are unique, such as doing CPR on a pregnant woman. When such a woman suffers cardiac arrest, you should be considering the welfare of two lives and not one. Irrespective of her pregnancy status, a woman who is pregnant and suffers cardiac arrest should be given CPR, and the process ought to follow normal or standard steps. You need to make sure the patient receives sufficient compressions, and, in addition, if you deem it necessary, uterus displacement that is manual is performed.

Dealing with Opioid Overdose

It has become common in present-day society to see patients who have overdosed on opioids, and there are families who keep naloxone in their homes just in case a vulnerable family member overdoses. Although in such circumstances it is important to know about time, dosage and route, ultimately CPR should be the procedure you think of first even as you make use of naloxone. For a better understanding of how to handle an opioid overdose emergency, you need to read about opioids and naloxone as well as displacement of the uterus in a manual way.

Need for Family Support

A fundamental way to assist families who find themselves in an emergency situation is establishment and maintenance of communication regarding the patient, as long as such communication is carried out between the medical personnel and the suitable people. You need to provide relevant family members with information that is factual, clear and also concise. Members from the emergency team should create rapport and trust between the family and medical staff. Such trust can be built by routinely providing patient updates.

You also need to pinpoint one member of the family whom you deem suitable to provide information and help other family members who may be very upset. In case death occurs on the scene and the dead patient is yet to be removed, communication is most helpful when given directly in private to family members. It is advisable that you read further on emergency impact, both psychological as well as medical, in times of emergency.

Education Necessary for EMTs & the Public

It is incumbent on individual EMTs to ensure they keep up-to-date with CPR skills and utilize available resources to learn more about emergency handling so that they are always confident in employing their skills. It is also important to educate the public whenever possible because having lay people who have the necessary CPR skills is bound to enhance rates of survival in times of emergency. It is a good idea, as an EMT, to actively help educate your local community on how to handle emergency situations. You need to read further about updates regarding CPR as well as community education.

Chapter 9: Pharmacology in Emergencies

The term 'pharmacology' is used in reference not only to ingredients and their preparation but also to actions different medications perform within the body. As an EMT, you need to understand the basics of pharmacology, including the way medication is administered.

How Medication Works

When patients are given medications, the intention is to minimize their pain while treating the ailment or infection that has affected them. Medications work differently based on the particular drug or drugs they contain. Overall, medication works by binding receptor cells from varying areas of a person's body, causing a particular effect like a raised heart rate or lessened pain.

When one speaks of a dose of medicine, what is meant is the amount of medicine given to a patient, while the medicine's therapeutic effect is the action that particular medicine ends up having on a person's body. However, there are times when a medication can have an unfavorable effect, and such unwanted effects are termed 'side effects.'

Names of Medications

Sometimes medications are called by their respective brand names while other times they are called by their generic names. Whenever you want to document a name that is generic, you usually write that name without capitalization. However, when you want to document the medicine using its brand name, which is basically the trade name or the name originating from the manufacturer, you should always capitalize that name.

For example, 'ibuprofen' is generic and its brand name is 'Advil.' Apart from the brand versus generic classification of medicines, there is also the classification of over-the-counter medicine versus prescription medicine. The former means you are allowed to buy it without any prescription from a doctor, while the latter means you can only buy it with an order from a doctor.

Routes of Medication Administration

You can use different means to administer medication, one of them being oral. This one is the most common all and is used when taking pills and many types of liquid medicine. Another route is injection, which directs medication either under the patient's skin or into a person's muscle.

As for medications of a respiratory nature, they are usually administered via inhalation. Other routes used to administer medication include 'sublingual,' meaning putting the medicine under the person's tongue; 'rectal,' meaning administering the medicine through the person's rectum and 'transcutaneous,' meaning administering medication via the patient's skin.

Medication Forms

Different medicines are packaged in varying forms, including liquid, tablet and capsule. There are also medications that come in the form of solutions easily administered to a patient via injection or IV. Other medications come in the form of gels and lotions, while others are creams, patches or gases.

The Process of Medication Administration

As an EMT, you should only administer the medication within your practice scope. Ensure you adhere to a particular process as you administer medication so that mistakes are avoided. This adherence is termed 'six rights of medication administration.'

One of those rights is to ensure you are administering medication to the correct patient. Another one is ensuring you are administering medication that is correct. Other rights include ensuring you give patients the right dose of medicine via the right route at the correct time. The sixth right is ensuring you have the correct documentation. If you fail to verify any of the stated factors you can end up causing an error in the administration of the medicine, which can sometimes cause life-threatening consequences.

Medication Administration by an EMT

Among the medications EMTs can administer is oxygen, given in gas form. EMTs are allowed to administer oral glucose as well as aspirin, and they can also administer epinephrine as well as activated charcoal. EMTs are also permitted to help a patient in the delivery of a metered-dose inhaler.

Medication Errors

There are varying types of medication errors, one of them being the administration of an incorrect dose. Another is medication administration via the wrong route. Errors pertaining to medication sometimes include administering medication that does not fall within your scope of medical practice, while errors pertaining to knowledge sometimes entail providing medication that is not right considering the health condition the patient needs to be treated for.

In case an error happens, it is important that you tell the truth about the whole issue. You need to give whatever medical assistance you deem necessary for the patient for the sake of preventing any adverse reaction. It is also important that you get in touch with the medical control department to let them know of the particular mistake and then adhere to your agency's policy in reporting and documenting that error in medication. To understand this concept even better, it is advisable to read further on nebulizers and nitroglycerin, dose inhalers that are metered and epinephrine as well as medication absorption.

Regarding Toxicology

Toxicology is the area of study that covers toxic substances, and EMTs need to understand it because they sometimes come across patients who have either been exposed to poison or who have ingested it.

Identifying Patients Affected By Poison

The first thing you should do is to establish if the patient has had contact with poison, either as a matter of being poisoned or being exposed to a toxin. Note that people who have been affected by poison sometimes develop varying symptoms, some of them similar to those that show up in medical ailments, and as such it is crucial that you are thorough in assessing the patient.

Poison Types

There are different ways by which poisons and other toxins could enter a person's body, and the types of poisons and toxins are varied. Some are in gas form, others liquid and yet others are solid. Also, poisons can gain entry into a person's body via different routes such as ingestion or absorption, inhalation or injection. However, the most common of all those routes is ingestion.

How to Assess a Patient

Once you are at the emergency scene, you need to first of all assess it to ensure it is safe, and also ensure there are no substances of a toxic nature that could present a danger to anyone, including the emergency team. Emergency conditions arising out of poisoning can be life-threatening, and so your primary duty is to assess the patient's airway and breathing as well as circulation.

You then need to record the history of the patient as you try to establish the timing of the poisoning, which could also be of use when eliminating other medical issues. When carrying out an assessment at a secondary level, you should ensure to assess the patient's vital signs and check if the patient is showing any poisoning signs that are not life-threatening. Your patient's state could change fast depending on the kind of poison or toxin involved, so you should keep reassessing the patients on an ongoing basis.

Emergency Care in Poisoning Incidences

When offering emergency assistance in cases of poisoning, you need to focus on providing support until your patient reaches the hospital. In many instances, administration of antidotes as well as extra treatment is given within the setting of a hospital, but emergency care needs to focus on the patient's airway as you monitor the patient closely.

Poisons Sometimes Underrated

Often people do not consider alcohol and drugs as poison, yet they can at times have adverse effects on a person's body. Opioids have the capacity to reduce a person's respiratory function, and the same case applies to synthetic drugs sold on the street. The danger is that a drastic reduction of the respiratory system's capacity can lead to cardiac arrest.

Other poisonous substances that could cause complications of a cardiac nature are chemicals that are inhaled like the ones some people use to get the feeling of being high, including those found in paint thinners and different cleaning products.

About Food Poisoning

You may encounter cases of food poisoning in the course of your work, and you need to be aware of the symptoms that include fever, diarrhea, vomiting and also stomach cramps. Bacteria capable of causing food poisoning include staphylococcus and salmonella as well as Escherichia coli. Food poisoning symptoms can manifest anywhere from two hours after consuming contaminated food that is contaminated to 12 hours later.

About Plant Poisoning

Poisoning through plants is also possible, and many times it affects children. There are various household plants that are poisonous, and if a child eats them, as they often put inedible things in the mouth, they could suffer poisoning. There are various life-threatening symptoms associated with plant poisonings, such as rashes on the skin as well as respiratory problems and others of a circulatory nature. Once you encounter such a case out in the field, you need to try and find out the exact plant the patient ingested and pass that information on to the medical staff at the hospital. To be better prepared for the NREMT exam, you need to read further on toxins and poisons and also antidotes, as well as material safety data sheets and hematemesis.

Psychiatric Emergencies

The category of emergencies of a psychiatric nature includes situations that can be life-threatening, such as attempts at suicide. A person can develop emotional crises of extreme degrees or extreme crises of a behavioral nature, both calling for medical attention.

Emotional Crisis

What can be termed a mental ailment is a condition affecting a person's ability to think and behave normally, and also affects the person's mood. Mental ailments can be exemplified by bipolar disorder as well as depression.

Crises of an emotional nature sometimes entail intense reactions, and individuals in an emotional crisis can also have a mental ailment underneath. Both of these conditions have the potential to interfere with a person's capacity to functional as normal.

Behavioral Crises

A behavioral crisis about someone's reaction to a given event or a situation. The person's reaction may be very intense in a way that ends up affecting the ability of that person to function as normal. Someone in a behavioral crisis could show signs of aggression while also being agitated, and such a person may also prove to be uncooperative. In fact, there are instances where the person's behavior can be so bizarre that they become dangerous not only to themselves but also to others.

About Pathophysiology Involving Behavioral Crises

There are two categorizations of behavioral crisis, or what are often termed 'psychiatric emergencies': organic and functional. Conditions under the organic classification are of a physical nature and occur as a consequence of a disturbance affecting the tissues of the brain.

Conditions under the functional classification arise following a disturbance in the way the affected person functions, with there being no sign of a physical trigger.

How to Approach Cases of Behavioral Crisis Safely

People undergoing a psychiatric emergency are normally unpredictable. It is of critical importance to follow an approach with the potential to help the patient while not causing them to feel threatened.

When approaching the person you intend to help, it is important to identify yourself first, and then to use language that is clear as you maintain a safe distance. You also need to be honest to the person even as you reassure them and maintain your calm. You should refrain from arguing with such a person, or you will escalate the situation.

How to Assess a Behavioral Crisis Patient

When you find yourself dealing with a psychiatric emergency case, it is important for you to assess whether you need support from law enforcement officers. When speaking to the patient, begin by explaining everything you intend to do as part of your primary assessment, so that you do not end up agitating the person.

Under the circumstances, it may be difficult to accurately document the patient's history, but you can try to get crucial information from members of the family who are at the scene. You need to do another assessment at a secondary level, where you closely observe the person concerned, trying to see if there is any change as far as the initial status is concerned, such as if the person looks more agitated than before.

Acute Psychosis Constituting an Emergency

One of the characteristics of acute psychosis is delusional behavior. People suffering from acute psychosis are normally not in touch with reality. Sometimes they see or hear things that are in no way real. Different reasons why people suffer acute psychosis include mental ailments like schizophrenia or drug use, and in some cases stress at extreme levels.

About Excited Delirium

Sometimes people can suffer what is referred to as 'excited delirium,' whose main characteristic is impairment of a person's cognitive ability. Sometimes such people experience hallucinations and are disoriented. Owing to the hallucinations, a person might begin to show signs of paranoia, and this has the potential for making the environment unsafe.

A person suffering excited delirium often manifests symptoms of sweating and heightened heart rate, and the pupils become dilated.

Need to Restrain Patient

In some cases, patients in excited delirium are a real risk not only to themselves but also to other people, and this danger could necessitate the patient being restrained. Such restraining should be effected only if the patient has the potential to cause harm to the EMTs or other members of the emergency team, people around them or themselves.

When it comes to the issue of restraint, the protocol followed varies from one EMS to another. Nevertheless, you need to always consider your own safety as you try to restrain a patient, and make sure you adhere to your agency's particular protocol.

Potential for Violence

Sometimes EMTs come into contact with patients who are violent, and so you need to assess the existence of any such risk in emergency situations. One of the ways to do this is to find out if the patient has a history involving violent acts. Next, you need to do an assessment of the person's body language as you seek to identify signs pointing to physical tension or aggression.

Evaluate what kind of speech the person is using as well as the language, noting elements like shouting. It is of great importance to be aware of your environment in order to determine whether there could be something close by that the person could utilize as a weapon. If ever you discern the potential for aggression or violence, you need to be extremely cautious and call for law enforcement to intervene as necessary.

Crises of an Emotional Nature

Suicide Attempts

EMTs sometimes encounter people suffering emotional crises and who are threatening to commit suicide, and if that is the case you need to take such threat seriously. Becoming tearful and showing signs of hopelessness are some of the signs a person might be suicidal.

Such people often manifest what is termed a 'flat effect' as well as an inability to face other people directly, and all these point to despair. You need to approach such a person calmly while organizing for law enforcement officers to bring backup.

About PTSD

PTSD stands for 'Post Traumatic Stress Disorder,' and it often develops after a person has experienced an extremely stressful situation like a serious motor accident or an assault or natural calamity. Often a person who has PTSD is not easy to predict, and the chances of them becoming upset fast are high. Some signs to look out for when trying to assess if someone has PTSD are anxiety, fear and an exaggerated response to being startled.

When trying to assist a person who has PTSD, it is important that you explain all that you intend to do pertaining to their situation, and make sure you give the explanation before starting. Avoid touching the person before seeking their permission, and keep maintaining a calm demeanor as you reassure them.

Pertaining to Legal Issues

When you encounter a patient who is not mentally competent, keep in mind the need to take into account considerations of legal nature. For one, if a patient is not mentally stable, you cannot expect them to consent to medical assistance on their own. At the same time, a patient who is not mentally competent could have officers of the law put them in protective custody, and that would enable EMTs and other medical personnel to provide medical treatment.

It is advisable for EMTs to involve officers of the law when dealing with patients who are not mentally competent. To understand these concepts better, you need to read further on acute psychosis and organic brain syndrome, PTSD and schizophrenia, as well as excited delirium.

Chapter 10: About Gynecological Emergencies

The anatomy of a woman and her physiology are quite complex, and often emergencies of a gynecological nature occur, affecting women from any age group. Some of the disorders that lead to emergencies affect ovaries, others the fallopian tubes, while others affect the uterus.

About Gynecological Anatomy & Physiology

The genitals of a female comprise the external parts that are inclusive of the 'labia majora' as well as 'labia minora.' It is possible for a female's labia to be easily injured as they are immensely vascular. The internal parts of these genitals are inclusive of the ovaries and uterus as well as the fallopian tubes.

Gynecological Pathophysiology

There are some conditions of a gynecological nature that sometimes turn into emergencies, such as when a woman has been subjected to trauma or has some form of infection. These conditions can be exemplified by pelvic inflammatory disease, abnormal vaginal bleeding or sexually transmitted diseases.

How to Assess a Patient with a Gynecological Emergency

Considering bleeding is a common factor in cases of gynecological emergency, you need to take precautionary measures as you assess the emergency scene. In case your patient has been sexually molested, you need to try and find an EMT who is female to render needed care. At the same time, you need to alert the police about the incident.

As you undertake a primary assessment, you need to establish the amount of blood the patient is likely to have lost to the extent of rendering her unstable. Also at the time of recording the history of the patient, you need to consider posing questions related to the possibility the patient might be pregnant. For example, inquire into the last date the woman had her menstrual period.

Then, when assessing the patient at the secondary level, it is important that you find out if the patient may have additional injuries, especially if you are dealing with a case of sexual molestation. You also need to check the patient's vital signs and mental condition, as well as any tenderness of the abdomen. It is important to keep reassessing the patient, frequently measuring her blood pressure, because cases that involve loss of blood are sensitive.

Gynecological Emergency Care

You need to safeguard the privacy of the patient as much as possible as you treat her, and let a female EMT tend to her whenever one is available. Bleeding could be a concern in emergencies of a gynecological nature, so you need to be alert in case you see any sign of shock since that would require appropriate treatment.

It is also important to be aware of the fact that genital injuries can be extremely painful. The area experiences intense pain because it is rich in nerve fibers. Lacerations should be treated using dressings that have been sterilized, and you should not try to extract any foreign bodies from the patient's vagina while giving emergency treatment out in the field.

How to Manage Gynecological Emergencies

When a specific gynecological problem has been identified, it is important to treat it in a particular manner, although there are instances where the assistance provided away from a hospital environment is, inevitably, limited. You could have a case, for instance, were a patient has pelvic inflammatory disease, but the best you can do as part of an emergency team in the field is manage pain and monitor the patient as you transport her.

If you are called to give emergency care in a pre-hospital setting and the patient has been sexually molested, the care you are expected to provide entails doing a thorough assessment of the patient's injuries, ensuring bleeding is under control and then offering support to the patient. You and your team should be sensitive to the nature of the emergency and show consideration as you handle the situation.

It is also important to involve the police in such cases, to provide guidance on how best to preserve evidence in addition to other forms of possible support. In order to be well prepared to correctly answer NREMT exam questions, it is advisable that you read further on chlamydia and the perineum, pelvic inflammatory disease and the cervix, as well as ovulation.

Regarding Obstetrics & Neonatal Care

Matters of obstetrics as well as neonatal health care relate to women before, during and after pregnancy, and also during childbirth. You therefore need to understand several conditions with the potential to adversely affect pregnant women and their babies.

Reproductive Anatomy & Physiology of a Woman

It is important to learn gynecological anatomy to be in a position to understand the reproductive system of a woman.

Once women reach childbearing age, their ovaries begin to release eggs, one every month, and the process through which this happens is referred to as ovulation. Once the egg is released, it moves down the female's fallopian tube, making itself available to be fertilized. If the egg is fertilized, it then gets implanted within the uterine wall's lining, where it grows into an embryo and continues developing to become a fetus.

In the meantime there is a placenta also developing, providing the fetus with nutrients as well as oxygen as it grows. There is an umbilical cord attached to the fetus and placenta, and that fetus is within an amniotic sac containing fluid meant to serve as its cushion.

How to Handle Normal Pregnancy

A pregnancy that is normal is expected to last around 40 weeks, although a baby who is born at 39 weeks of gestation is considered to be full-term. The period of pregnancy is split into three equal trimesters. In a normal pregnancy, many changes happen inside the body of the woman, one of them being increased blood volume. Other changes include weight gain, slowing down of digestive functions and joints loosening due to hormones associated with the pregnancy.

Complications During Pregnancy

Complications associated with pregnancy fall in a wide range, beginning from some that are minor to others that are serious and a potential threat to the lives of mother and baby. Among complications associated with pregnancy is gestational diabetes, an ailment that affects a mother as the pregnancy progresses. Another one is bleeding of the uterus, and this can be caused by different factors. One of those causes could be problems with the placenta. Another problem during pregnancy is preeclampsia, a complication involving a woman developing heightened blood pressure.

Trauma in Pregnancy

When a pregnant woman experiences trauma, she may incur injuries that affect both her and her unborn baby, and considering the woman has a high volume of blood, she could end up bleeding excessively during injury. It is important that you take special care in handling a pregnant woman when trauma has impacted the area of her abdomen. In case the woman has had trauma to her abdomen, there is bound to be bleeding from her vagina as well as pain in the abdominal region.

You also need to understand that the injuries a pregnant woman sustains during a car accident could be from seat belts that were worn incorrectly. As such, it is important that you carry out your assessment at the scene of the emergency properly.

Values Associated With Culture

There are some differences in culture that lead to women dealing with their pregnancy differently, and EMTs, as well as paramedics, need to take those differences into account and respect them when assisting the patients. For instance, women in some cultures do not welcome being handled by male EMTs or other make health-care givers, so if you encounter such a situation, it is important that you try to let an EMT who is female assist the patient if that is possible under the circumstances.

When Teens are in Pregnancy-Related Emergencies

While it is true every pregnancy is unique, there are complications that are generally associated with teenagers, and one of them is a high rate of teenagers giving birth to underweight babies. Any time you are giving treatment to a pregnant teenager, it is important that you try to involve the parents. You also need to understand the laws governing the particular state the emergency is in with regard to a teenager's ability to decline care independently. There are several states where a pregnant teenager's rights are the same as those of adults insofar as medical assistance is concerned.

How to Assess a Pregnant Patient

Any time you are about to approach a location where there is a pregnant woman involved, you need to take your time and exercise standard precautions. Even if you find members of the family who are anxious, avoid being influenced into rushing as you assess the scene.

In your primary assessment, try to establish whether the pregnant patient is actually experiencing active labor, and then assess whether there is a likelihood of other potential problems. You need to assess if she has difficulty breathing or if she is bleeding. Also, when taking the woman's history, find out how far along the pregnancy is and whether she has experienced any pregnancy-related problems.

Then, as you assess the woman at a secondary level, find out if the fetus is moving and if all vital signs of a maternal nature are present. It is also crucial that you watch for signs of dropping blood pressure because that could indicate bleeding. Make sure you reassess the pregnant woman on a frequent basis as you monitor her to note any changes associated with her vital signs.

How to Handle Emergency Normal Delivery

Whenever a pregnant woman has a normal delivery, there are three stages of labor involved, namely dilating of the woman's cervix, delivering the baby and delivering the placenta. An EMT called to handle an emergency situation where a woman is about to undergo normal delivery should keep monitoring the woman as she is transported to a medical facility.

However, there are cases that do not allow for the pregnant woman to be transported to a hospital to deliver her baby there, and in such cases, the EMT should be prepared to handle the delivery.

If you are faced with such a situation, open your obstetrical kit (OB kit) and ensure the woman is positioned properly and ready to deliver in privacy. Check for crowning, where the head of the baby is right at the mother's vaginal opening. You need to provide support for the head of the baby as the woman pushes and the head of the baby emerges.

It is also important to check if the baby's neck is surrounded by the umbilical cord, and if that is the case, you should lift the umbilical cord carefully above the head of the baby. After successful delivery of the baby's head, the baby should onto one side just as you deliver the shoulders, and following delivery of the shoulders, the rest of the baby's body will emerge.

Post-Delivery in Normal Delivery

Once you have helped deliver the baby, put the young one carefully on her mother's chest so as to give them skin-to-skin contact. After that, dry the newborn using a towel and wrap it in a clean, dry blanket. Clamp the umbilical cord immediately after it has stopped pulsating.

Labor ends when the placenta is delivered, and this usually happens on its own, with the EMT required to render only a little help. You could help in delivering the placenta just a couple of minutes after the birth of a newborn, but if this is not the case just transport the woman to the required medical institution and the placenta can be delivered in due course. In short, failure for the placenta to be delivered should not be a reason to delay the woman's transportation to a hospital setting.

Neonatal Care during Emergency

The initial steps you should take in caring for the newborn baby are related to keeping the baby warm and dry. You may also wish to suction the mouth and nose of the baby if you see secretions present. It is also important that you carry out an assessment of the baby so as to establish if it requires resuscitation, and you accomplish this by evaluating the baby's breathing and tone of its muscles as well as its heart rate.

In case the newborn does not cry, initiate stimulation by flicking the baby's soles. If even after the feet flicking, the baby still does not cry, there is a need for more serious intervention, and resuscitation may be one of them, carrying out manual ventilation and chest compressions.

Delivery-Related Emergencies

Complications associated with delivery are varied, and breech delivery is one of the most prevalent complications that constitute an emergency. In normal cases, newborns come out with their heads first, but in cases of a breech, the baby's feet or butt emerge first. Babies in such situations are at risk of some form of trauma during delivery. Another complication that could arise is having the umbilical cord being prolapsed, meaning the umbilical cord precedes the baby on the way out. For any pregnant woman anticipating a complicated delivery, it is important to alert the 'Advanced Cardiovascular Life Support' (ACLS) for backup.

Complications That Arise Post-Delivery

Emergencies can arise following complications that develop after the mother has delivered her newborn baby, and the one considered most common is bleeding. Obviously, some level of bleeding is expected during childbirth and soon after, but it is not the kind of bleeding that occurs when the mother's uterus fails to begin contracting. If uterus contraction does not begin as anticipated, the mother can have excessive bleeding that can cause life-threatening complications.

Use a sterile pad to absorb the blood being lost and begin administering oxygen to the mother as you transport her right away to a hospital. To understand these concepts better, you need to read further on abruption placenta and the birth canal, preeclampsia and meconium, the Apgar score and term gestation as well as lightening.

Chapter 11: Medical Terminologies Used in Emergencies

It is crucial for EMTs to understand the medical terminologies frequently used in emergency situations, so as to be able to have effective conversations with other medical personnel.

How Medical Terms are Formed

Medical terms comprise varying parts, inclusive of the root and suffix as well as the prefix. There is also room to change a part of the medical term, hence altering the entire meaning of that term.

The root is the word's foundation and is found in most of the medical terms you come across. The prefix is the part of the word that precedes the root, while the suffix follows the root. Often the role of the prefix in a medical term is to describe a location. If you take the example of the term 'tonsillitis,' the root is 'tonsil,' while the term's suffix is 'itis.' You need to learn more about words commonly used as roots in the medical field, particularly in emergency situations, as well as their prefixes and suffixes.

Notation Shortcuts

Sometimes even when EMTs, paramedics and other medical personnel know the actual medical terms, they choose to use abbreviations, symbols and acronyms. Knowing how to use these short forms makes for easier, faster communication, as long as those abbreviations you use are legible and accurate. If you take the example of symbols that represent 'post,' 'right' or 'left,' you would be faster if you used their respective symbols in place of the full words.

However, abbreviations and symbols sometimes vary from one agency to another, so you need to be certain that the short form you are using has been approved under the agency you are working with, and also as you use those short forms in your documentation.

Terms Involving Movement & Direction

There are several terms you can use to describe direction and different movements. Some of these include 'superior,' 'inferior,' 'medial' and 'lateral.' The term 'superior' as a medical term means closest to the person's head, and 'inferior' used as a medical term means nearest to the person's feet. Meanwhile, 'medial' is used as a medical term to mean a part of a person's body that is in close proximity to the body's middle. 'Lateral,' as a medical term, means some distance away from the body's middle. To understand these concepts better, you need to read further on proximal and distal, apex and flexion, superficial and extension, as well as anterior and posterior.

The Human Body

Understanding the anatomy of a human being is crucial to provide the right treatment for a patient and give the right information to hospital staff.

About Topographical Anatomy

The human body can be divided into separate planes, and this enables medical staff to describe patients' symptoms and injuries with relative ease. If you imagine a split that ranges from the front and cuts to the back, what you get are 'frontal planes,' and when you imagine a split of the body of the body beginning the top all the way to the bottom, you have 'transverse planes.' Then you have the split that divides the human body into the right side and the left side, thus creating the 'lateral plane.' In order to understand this area better, it is advisable to read further on the coronal and axial planes and the sagittal and mid-sagittal planes.

Skeletal System's Anatomy & Physiology

The body's skeletal symptom, which comprises the bones and ligaments as well as cartilages and tendons, has two sections, one of them being referred to as 'appendicular' and the other one 'axial.' The appendicular skeletal system comprises the pelvis, legs and arms, while the axial skeletal system comprises the skull, facial bones, thoracic cage and vertebra. To understand these areas better, you need to read further on the ligaments and tendons, the cartilage and cranium, the thorax and the vertebrae, the femur and the tibia and also the pelvis.

The Musculoskeletal System's Anatomy and Physiology

A person's musculoskeletal system provides form to the body while also protecting vital organs. There are also muscle tissues that are crucial in facilitating movement. Within the musculoskeletal system are the voluntary muscle tissue as well as bones, the muscle tissue comprising three types that include the 'cardia' that is linked to a person's heart; the 'smooth muscle' that is attached to a person's vessels blood vessels and intestines; and the 'skeletal' that is attached to a person's bones. You need to read further about the voluntary muscle as well as the involuntary muscle.

Respiratory System Anatomy & Physiology

As discussed earlier, a person's respiratory system is normally divided into two parts, namely the 'upper' and 'lower' airway. The upper airway is made up of the nose and mouth as well as the jaw, larynx and the pharynx. As for the lower airway, it comprises the bronchus as well as the lungs. One of the roles of the upper airway is to warm and humidify the air that passes through. In the meantime, a person's lower airway plays its role in the exchange of gases, and that includes enabling oxygen to enter the lungs and carbon dioxide to leave.

As a whole, the respiratory system enables ventilation that moves air in and out of a person's lungs, as well as respiration that is simply the exchange of gases. It is important that you read further on the concepts of nasopharynx and trachea, epiglottis and diaphragm, thyroid and cartilage, pleura and alveoli, as well as ventilation and respiration.

Circulatory System Anatomy & Physiology

The body's circulatory system works not only with the arteries and veins but also with capillaries and the heart. All these organs help in transportation of blood all over a person's body. Another term used in reference to the circulatory system is the 'cardiovascular system,' and it comprises the pulmonary circulation as well as the systemic circulation and its two major divisions.

The role of the systemic circulation is to carry the blood rich in oxygen out of the heart and to the rest of the body and then carry it back to the heart. Pulmonary circulation's role is to transport blood that has minimal oxygen out of the heart and into the lungs so that it can collect oxygen from the lungs and then return to the heart rich in oxygen. It is important that you read further about the myocardium and ventricular, the pulmonary veins and the atrium, stroke volume and cardiac output and also capillaries and perfusion.

Nervous System Anatomy & Physiology

A person's nervous system comprises the spinal cord, nerves and brain. It is the system responsible for nearly all the other systems of the body. For instance, it is the nervous system that controls the fundamental functions of regulation of temperature and blood pressure as well as breathing. The system is divided into two sections, namely, the 'central nervous system,' comprising the brain and the spinal cord and the 'peripheral system' that comprises the nerves that exist outside the person's spine and brain. You need to read further in order to understand the nervous system as well as the somatic nervous system, the automatic nervous system, brain stem and also the sensory and motor nerves.

Digestive System Anatomy & Physiology

A person's digestive system plays the role of breaking down food consumed and supplying nutrients and calories to the body. The gastrointestinal system includes organs that are hollow such as the intestines and the stomach, as well as the bladder. In case the hollow organs are perforated, there is the danger of waste matter spilling into the abdominal cavity and causing infection. The solid organs forming part of the gastrointestinal system are the spleen and the pancreas, as well as the kidneys and liver. You need to read also about the salivary glands and retroperitoneal as well as chyme and the bile ducts.

Lymphatic System Anatomy & Physiology

A person's lymphatic system is supportive of both the circulatory and immune systems, and it also helps in the removal of fluid from tissues even as it carries white blood cells and plays the role of absorbing fatty acids. It is responsible for removing toxins as well as waste matter from a person's body. A person's lymphatic system comprises the lymph nodes and thymus glands as well as lymph vessels and glands. It is advisable to read further on the lymph nodes and the lymph fluid.

Urinary System Anatomy & Physiology

A person's urinary system is responsible for the removal of waste matter from the kidneys, and also controls fluid balance even as it helps in the maintenance of appropriate blood pH. This system is made up of two kidneys, bladder, ureters and the urethra. The kidneys are the organs responsible for filtering of waste matter from a person's blood, while the ureters, which are hollow and tube-like, carry the waste in liquid form out of the kidneys and into the bladder. The liquid waste is stored in the bladder until a person urinates. The urethra is responsible for carrying the urine out of the bladder and out of the body. You need to read about peristalsis as well as the renal pelvis.

Genital System Anatomy & Physiology

A person's genital system comprises all reproductive organs that are involved in the production of life. The anatomy of a male's reproductive system comprises the penis and testicles as well as the prostate gland, while the genital system of a female comprises the vagina and the ovaries, the fallopian tubes and cervix as well as the uterus. You need to read further on the ovaries and seminal vesicles, and also on the cervix and fallopian tubes.

Pathophysiology

The term 'pathophysiology' is used in reference to the effect a particular illness has on a person's physiological processes. EMTs are expected to take care of patients suffering from different medical conditions and illnesses, and these affect a person's systems in various ways. A good example is an illness that causes respiratory problems such as asthma, COPD or pneumonia which compromise a person's respiratory function.

A person might also contract a disease that interferes with multiple organs or body systems, as opposed to just one. A good example is shock. You need to read more about shock, cellular respiration and respiratory compromise.

Life-Span Development

The term 'Life Span-Development' is used in reference to changes occurring from when a person is born to the time that person dies. EMTs are encouraged to learn about life-span development thoroughly so that they are able to treat patients across all age groups appropriately.

Neonates and Infants

Any baby is taken to be a 'neonate' the minute it is born until it attains the age of one month. From one month to one year, a baby is referred to as an infant. Medical personnel provide appropriate ways of treating an infant that vary from the treatment given to an adult.

One of the reasons that necessitates such variations in treatment has to do with the respiratory rate and heart rate. A baby's respiratory rate and heart rate are, in normal cases, faster the younger that baby is. It is also important to know that babies generally confine their breathing to the nose and have airways that are smaller the younger they are. This makes an infant more vulnerable to obstruction of the airway than an older child or adult.

Toddlers and Preschoolers

The term 'toddler' is used in reference to a child who is one year to three years old, while the term 'preschooler' is used in reference to a child who is three years to six years old. Although children within this age range have respiratory and heart rates that are faster than adults, theirs are still slower than those of infants.

Toddlers are known to be prone to separation anxiety, and the rate at which they develop language varies. This category of children is prone to accidents, and many accidental deaths happen when children within this age category.

School-Age Children

'School-age children' is a term used in reference to children whose age falls within six years to 12 years. The vital signs of these children are only a bit faster compared to those of adults. Children in this age bracket are concerned about being accepted by their peers.

When you are treating children in the school-age category, ensure you explain the procedures you intend to follow so that they can understand whatever is happening to them. This is likely to reduce any fear or anxiety they have, meaning the treatment can be expedited.

Adolescents

The term 'adolescents' is used in reference to children whose age ranges from 13 to 18 years. Often, when it comes to matters of a medical nature, adolescents are given the same treatment as adults, although there are instances where medication is given on the basis of a person's weight as opposed to their age. Considering how varied development among adolescents can be, it is crucial that you rely on the size of the adolescent as opposed to their age. When it comes to fatalities, accidents are the leading cause among adolescents.

Early Adults

The term 'early adults' is used in reference to people whose age is from 19 years to 40 years. In this period, you are likely to find that individuals are at their physical peak.

Normally the vital signs of people within this age group are similar to when they enter their middle adulthood, although there are some changes that usually occur as the end of early adulthood approaches. Some of those changes include a person losing their muscle mass while increasing their body fat. Their reflexes also become slower. In fact, inadvertent injuries are some of the top causes of death among people in this age category.

Middle Adults

The term 'middle adults' is used in reference to people whose age falls within the range beginning at 41 years to 60 years. However, for some people middle adulthood may appear to begin earlier due to the onset of problems of a medical nature, for example, diabetes and cardiovascular illness as well as vision and hearing impairment, which are normally associated with middle adulthood.

Adults whose age is within the 41 to 44 range are prone to inadvertent injuries, and such injuries are a leading cause of death in that age group. For those whose age is within the range of 45 to 60, cancer leads other causes of death.

Older Adults

The term 'older adults' is used in reference to people who have attained the age of 61 years. There are various medical issues associated with people of this age category, many of them chronic in nature. COPD, heart diseases and others are some of those diseases likely to affect older adults more than people who are younger. The leading cause of death among older adults 65 years and below is still cancer, while the leading cause of death after adults have passed the age of 65 is heart disease. You need to read more on fontanelles and pre-conventional reasoning as well as life expectancy.

Neurological Emergencies

The term 'neurological emergencies' is used in reference to conditions associated with the brain. Some neurological issues could be life-threatening. People of all ages can find themselves in neurological emergencies, although adults are more affected.

Neurological Anatomy & Physiology

A person's brain has divisions, and the segments into which it is divided include the brainstem, cerebrum and cerebellum. Each of these segments has a function to control. For example, there is a specific area of the brain that controls speech, breathing, sight, moving and swallowing.

A person's brain also works through a complex nerve network whose main role is to transport messages from the brain to different areas of an individual's body.

Neurological Pathophysiology

Many issues of a neurological nature can arise, and while some are mild, others can be life-threatening. The symptoms of neurological emergencies depend on the segment of the brain that has been affected, and the faster that area can be identified, the easier it usually is to achieve positive outcomes after treatment.

Headache

The term 'headache' is used in reference to a neurological issue that is very prevalent, but which does not ordinarily signify a serious medical issue. That said, there are times when a headache can be a symptom of a serious medical condition such as in the case of meningitis or a stroke.

The origin of the pain causing a headache is not really the brain, considering a person's brain has no pain receptors, yet that pain is felt within the blood vessels, the scalp, meninges and other areas.

Stroke

The term 'stroke' is used in reference to a medical emergency that is serious and could cause death or permanent brain damage. A person suffers a stroke when the blood flowing into the brain is interrupted, in many instances due to a clot. During such interruption of blood flow, brain cells can begin dying, and the affected person can suffer temporary or permanent damage.

Some symptoms of a stroke include headache and confusion, as well as slurred speech. There are also other medical conditions that resemble a stroke, such as hypoglycemia, or another condition that develops following a seizure, termed 'postictal state.'

Seizures

The term 'seizure' is used in reference to activity of an electrical nature that happens within the brain. Some of the characteristics of this activity are a person's muscles becoming rigid and their activity being uncontrollable. There are instances where seizures result in a person losing consciousness.

Epilepsy is a leading cause of seizures, but seizures can also be caused by brain tumors, brain injury caused by trauma or drugs. During a seizure, it is important to manage the airway of the person affected so as to sustain life.

Altered Mental Status

The term 'altered mental status' is used in reference to a situation where a person cannot think with clarity. There are many conditions that can lead to such a state, and they include stroke and seizures, use of alcohol or drugs, injury to the brain, brain infection and hyperglycemia.

Patients with an 'altered mental status' require varying treatments, and so it is crucial to keep assessing the patient with a view to understanding the real cause of the person having an 'altered level of consciousness' (ALOC).

Patient Assessment

The term 'patient assessment' is used in reference to the evaluation carried out by EMTs on arrival at the scene of an emergency. They first assess how safe the scene is even before they begin treatment of any neurological emergency. After this, they do a survey with a view to determining if the patient has any condition that is life-threatening, and considering how easy it is for a neurological condition to interfere with breathing, it is important that EMTs also prioritize managing a patient's airway.

It is also important to record a patient's history that can provide an idea of the nature of the complication the medical staff needs to deal with. There is another survey the EMTs are expected to carry out at a secondary level, and this entails assessing the patient's vital signs as well as checking to see if the patient might have suffered a stroke. It is important to keep reassessing the patient from time to time on the way to the hospital because the status of neurological problems can change very fast.

Emergency Care

There are many conditions of a neurological nature, such as a stroke, which need to be treated within a hospital setting. As such, pre-hospital care is likely to be restricted to management of the patient's airway, and then the patient should be quickly transported to a medical facility. However, there are some situations where EMTs or other emergency staff can administer medication at the scene of an emergency, and a good example is a case of seizure.

There are medications meant to reduce the incidence of seizures. You need to read more on strokes and seizures, status epilepticus and ischemia, TIA, CVA and ALOC and also delirium.

Gastrointestinal Emergencies

Emergencies of a gastrointestinal or urologic nature usually affect a person's stomach or intestines, bladder or gallbladder, and they can affect other organs as well. Since the emergencies that can arise under this category fall within a wide range, it is very important that EMTs try and narrow down the medical issue as quickly as possible so that suitable treatment can be provided.

Pathophysiology Affecting the Gastrointestinal System

There are many conditions with the potential to affect a person's gastrointestinal system, and one of them is referred to as 'peritonitis.' This is a condition where material such as blood or pus ends up irritating the body's peritoneum.

EMTs in the field also frequently encounter cases of 'acute abdomen,' referring to an incidence of abdominal pain manifesting all of a sudden. This can happen for various reasons, among them appendicitis and gastroenteritis, as well as diverticulitis.

Patient Assessment

EMTs are expected to assess the emergency scene immediately on arrival, and then to complete their primary assessment of the patient. It is also important to be aware that there are gastrointestinal problems likely to cause bleeding internally, which could make the condition life-threatening.

One symptom that could be helpful in assessing the seriousness of the condition is declining blood pressure. EMTs should review the patient's history and conduct a further assessment at secondary level, as it will be of much help to learn the time the symptoms began and whether the patient had other symptoms such as vomiting or diarrhea.

The assessment being carried out at a secondary level should also involve checking if the abdomen has any palpitations or is tender. As an EMT you need to continue reassessing the patient as emergencies of a gastrointestinal nature have been known to quickly develop into more serious conditions, shock being one example.

Emergency Care

The term 'emergency care' is used in reference to care that is provided in the form of patient assessment and treatment on an emergency basis, particularly with regard to a patient who has suffered shock. In case the patient has vomited, for example, this could cause the airway to be compromised, and for that reason, EMTs should ensure patients are put in a position that will not interfere with the patency of their airway. When handling a vomiting patient, you need to protect yourself to avoid being contaminated.

Dialysis Emergencies

Dialysis emergencies pertain to patients who have renal illness that is in its last stage, meaning they may require dialysis. Dialysis is a process that performs the work the kidneys should have been doing because the kidneys are unable to function as expected. There are some instances where patients receiving dialysis experience unfavorable side effects and EMTs are permitted to treat such patients in emergency situations. Some side effects of dialysis that lead to emergencies include vomiting and bleeding at the site of access and infection. The care EMTs are expected to provide in such emergency situation entails assessment and management of the patient's airway, breathing and circulation.

Endocrine & Hematologic Emergencies

Endocrine and hematological emergencies entail emergency conditions caused by diabetes or disorders of the blood such as sickle cell anemia.

Endocrine Anatomy & Physiology

There are many bodily functions under the control of the endocrine system, which comprises glands such as the thyroid and pancreas, as well as the adrenal glands whose main role is to secrete hormones that affect cells forming different body organs. Sometimes the endocrine glands produce hormones in excess, yet one of the system's roles is the production of sufficient insulin to enable glucose to penetrate body cells and to serve as a source of energy.

Endocrine Pathophysiology

When the endocrine system does not function well, a person could develop diabetes, which is a condition involving impairment of the way glucose is metabolized in the body. Production of glucose could also be compromised, and in some instances, insulin might fail to bind the receptor cells in which case glucose will be deterred from entering the cells. Diabetes is a condition that can be life-threatening, and sometimes people with diabetes go into a coma, become blind or develop kidney disease.

Assessment of Diabetic Patients

When attending to a diabetic emergency, EMTs need to carry out an assessment of the scene in order to ensure the safety of everyone involved, and you need to be particularly careful in checking for the presence of any needles that may have been used to inject insulin. Since there is a chance of breathing becoming impaired as a result of a diabetic emergency, you need to carry out your primary assessment as soon as possible.

Assess how conscious the patient is, and take a careful medical history as this is particularly critical in diabetic patients. In the history, you need to include what the patient consumed before the incident and when he or she last had an insulin treatment.

After this, you need to do another assessment at a secondary level that involves checking the patient's vital signs as well as other possible symptoms. You also need to keep reassessing the patient even on the way to the hospital, so as to see if any changes in the patient's status have happened such as ALOC.

Diabetic Emergency Care

Diabetic emergency care mostly entails administration of oral glucose, which is normally administered in forms such as liquid, chewable tablets and gel. In many cases, EMTs use the gel form of oral glucose as it dissolves fast. The problem or contraindication when you choose this form of glucose administration arises if the patient is not in a position to swallow anything.

For patients with ALOC, it is advisable to put the gel on a tongue depressor before putting that depressor into the mouth of the patient in between the cheek and gums. You can also treat a diabetic patient for shock even as you manage the airway during an emergency.

Hypoglycemia

The term 'hypoglycemia' is used in reference to a low level of blood glucose, and it is crucial that you recognize hypoglycemia to be able to facilitate rapid, life-saving treatment. Signs you should look for to determine the patient has hypoglycemia include sweating and shakiness, confusion and blurred vision, rapid heart rate, seizures, lack of consciousness, ALOC and other symptoms.

It is important to keep in mind the reality that some of these symptoms, like ALOC and seizures, are also present when patients have different conditions other than hypoglycemia. Taking the patient's history even as you check blood sugar levels is very important when it comes to handling emergency cases of hypoglycemia.

Hematologic Emergencies

The term 'hematological emergencies' is used in reference to treatment provided to patients who have varying disorders of the blood, such as sickle cell anemia and hemophilia or thrombophilia. There are times when people with sickle cell anemia suffer organ damage while developing hypoxia, and also find themselves in a crisis of pain.

People who have hemophilia have blood which does not easily clot, and this can pose life-threatening problems especially if such people bleed internally or externally, and this includes bleeding from minor injuries. People with thrombophilia can easily develop clots in their blood, and this has the potential to obstruct the blood flow to the patient's vital organs.

Assessing Patients for Hematologic Disorders

Any time you want to treat a patient in a hematological emergency, it is important that you do an initial assessment to establish how safe the scene is. Also make a point of checking if there is any sign of blood around and use standard precautions as necessary. You will also need to protect your eyes. In the course of your primary assessment, you need to establish if the patient is conscious and what that level of consciousness is. You also need to establish if the patient's airway has been compromised.

The history of the patient can provide helpful information such as what the patient's hematological issue is like. If dealing with patients who have sickle cell disease, you can anticipate their pulse to be rapid but weak, and as such you need to monitor the patient's vital signs when doing your secondary assessment. Keep reassessing the person on a frequent basis so that you can note if any changes arise pertaining to alertness or level of oxygen. You need to read further on acidosis and sickle cell anemia, hematology and hemophilia and thrombophilia.

Immunological Emergencies

Emergencies of an immunological nature relate to allergic reactions, which can range from mild to very severe. Considering there is the potential for blockage of a person's airway during such an emergency, you need to assess for such blockage as soon as possible so as to avert a situation where the patient becomes unable to breathe.

Anatomy and Physiology

A person's immune system comprises lymph nodes and lymph vessels as well as the spleen and the bone marrow. The tissue and cells, as well as entire organs within the person's immune system, assist in fighting infection. It is the spleen that is responsible for killing bacteria, while an individual's bone marrow plays the role of producing cells; both red and white cells are great at fighting disease. The vessels and lymph nodes act as a trap for bacteria within body fluids, and the trapped bacteria is then cleared by the lymphocytes.

Pathophysiology

EMTs often treat immunological emergencies of an allergic nature, which usually occur when someone's body produces a response as though it has been exposed to something dangerous though the substance is generally harmless. In short, it is the person's immune system overreacting and releasing chemicals, such as histamine, which triggers symptoms like sneezing, hives or watery eyes.

The allergic complication considered most dangerous is referred to as anaphylaxis, and it is known to affect several organs, one of them being the respiratory system.

Allergens

Allergens can be divided into different categories, namely food and medications, chemicals, plants and insects. Allergens in the food category include shellfish, peanuts and milk. Penicillin is one example of an allergen in the medication category, while mold, oak, pollen and ragweed constitute allergens under the plant category. Under the chemical category are allergens such as latex, while bee and wasp stings constitute allergens in the insect category.

Assessing a Patient in an Immunological Emergency

A patient's airway may be blocked during an emergency of an immunological nature, and so you need to carry out your primary assessment as fast as possible. During this assessment, you should check if the person's airway is still patent as you evaluate the status of respiratory function. It is important to get the patient's history to learn if the person has had allergies in the past, before carrying out a secondary assessment to see if the vital signs, level of oxygen and breath sounds are normal.

Be aware that a patient's status can change fast during an immunological emergency, and therefore it's critical to keep reassessing the patient as you focus on the patency of the airway, consciousness level and rate of respiration.

Immunological Emergency Support

When handling an emergency of an immunological nature, you need to focus mainly on supporting the airway function and providing fast transportation to a medical facility. When the allergic reaction is severe, or in instances when there is anaphylaxis, there is a need to administer epinephrine at the scene. Epinephrine is known for reducing the swelling of the airway and bronchospasms of the lungs and improves blood flow, thereby providing fast treatment for anaphylaxis.

When treating an allergic reaction with epinephrine, you need to administer it using an auto-injector with a pre-measured dose. It will be helpful for you as you prepare to answer NREMT exam questions to read further on histamines and allergens, leukotrienes, anaphylaxis and angioedema.

Chapter 12: What You Need to Know About Trauma Emergencies

Very often, calls to EMS require EMTs to be skilled in handling trauma cases. In this chapter, you are going to learn the topics related to trauma which are often tested in the NREMT exam. Not only are you expected to learn the procedures, but also the terms used.

Trauma can be defined as grave physical and/or emotional damage. Such injury could be in the form of a wound that is visible, for example, an injury sustained during a motor accident, or in the form of an emotional reaction such as when a person has been a victim of rape. It is typical for a person who has been traumatized to experience shock and be in denial. You need to read in detail about emergencies associated with trauma.

Energy & Trauma

There are three energy types that are associated with people who have suffered injury, and understanding of Newton's Law of Motion in physics comes in handy. It makes it easy to understand how to carry out a patient's assessment of the physical aspect, thus enhancing your competency as well as proficiency. To understand this topic better, you need to read further on kinetic energy and work energy as well as potential energy, the impact of energy on an injury and Newton's Law of Motion.

How Injuries Happen

A person may suffer injuries in different ways, and therefore you should consider how an injured happened, what exactly happened, when it happened, and where. At the minimum, it is important that you consider three of these aspects of injury every time you want to treat a patient. For a better understanding of the topic, you need to read further on injury mechanism, significance and non-significance of an injury and multi-system injuries.

About Blunt Trauma

'Blunt trauma' is used in reference to two major trauma categories. One category is non-invasive, meaning it hardly breaks the skin barrier. However, this does not mean it cannot be serious. The reason such injuries sometimes turn out to be serious is the risk of internal bleeding or involvement of internal organs.

You need to read further on penetrating as well as blunt-force trauma, deceleration and injury mechanism, signs and symptoms, suspicion index, coup and contre-coup injuries of the brain.

About Penetrating Trauma

'Penetrating trauma' is the other trauma category, referring to an injury that penetrates a person's skin and often goes deeper. When a patient sustains penetrating trauma, not only can you see the external wounds, but also the internal ones. It is important for you to read further on injury mechanism and cavitation, trajectory and drag, signs and symptoms and suspicion index as well as projectiles.

About Blast Injuries

People suffer blast injuries in one of four ways—primary, a secondary, tertiary and quaternary. The major variations among the injury types are the occurrence mechanisms. A patient can sustain multiples types of blast injuries. You need to read more about pulmonary blast injuries and the tympanic membrane, arterial air embolisms and the four types of blast injuries.

About Multi-system Trauma

'Multi-system' trauma refers to injuries that involve multiple parts of the body. In such instances, you could be dealing with a patient whose situation is life-threatening. Sometimes it requires extensive care and an interdisciplinary team of medical staff. To be able to answer relevant NREMT questions, you need to read further on the golden principles and the golden hour or period.

About Patient Assessment

Assessing a patient involves gathering information required for use when addressing a patient's medical needs on the basis of the situation. When it comes to trauma, the process calls for organization and thoroughness as well as timeliness. You need to focus on identifying the patient's injuries by considering the major complaint and clues of a visual nature as well as vital signs. You also need to identify symptoms as you take into account the physical assessment.

In order to be well prepared to answer NREMT questions, you need to read further on patient assessment components, points of assessment specific to neck and throat injuries, as well as those associated with injuries of the head, abdomen and chest.

About Transportation & Destination

It is crucial for EMTs to appropriately utilize transportation resources and to know the levels of trauma centers. The main aim of any medical system handling emergencies is to enhance safety, treatment efficiency, quality and timeliness in the period preceding hospital care. This entails traveling using the most efficient transport mode and getting to a trauma center of the level that is most suitable on the basis of the patient's acuity.

You need to read more on how trauma centers are classified, 'Revised Trauma Score' (RTS), scene time, transport resource types, trauma score and related concepts.

Other Important Trauma Areas

In order to be well prepared to correctly answer NREMT exam questions about trauma, you need to review the workings of the cardiovascular system, pathophysiology and perfusion and external and internal bleeding. You should also pay close attention to standard precautions, how best to control bleeding, epistaxis and tourniquets, as well as hemostatic agents.

220 NREMT Exam Questions

(1) If you reach the site where a woman of advanced age has fallen and injured her ribs, and when you check you find she is breathing rapidly and shallowly, the rate being 40, how can you confirm that this emergency is life-threatening?

(A) There is the risk of her volume per minute being excessive

(B) There is the risk of her volume per minute diminishing

(C) Her limit for the air referred to as 'dead space' has been reached

(D) You can see her inhaling excessive oxygen

(2) EMTs normally use an endotracheal tube:

(A) To suction the patient's hypopharynx

(B) To insert in the patient's esophagus

(C) For insertion inside the patient's trachea

(D) To serve as an avenue for medication

(3) 'Sellick's maneuver' is meant for:

(A) Reducing vomiting risk

(B) Making the carina visible

(C) Making the vallecular visible

(D) Collapsing the patient's trachea

(4) Once you have the endotracheal tube in place, and as you perform auscultation, you realize the patient's right side has sounds from the lungs but the left does not, or they are minimal. What should be your next move?

(A) Extract the tube and try intubation again

(B) Abandon it and initiate respirations

(C) Ensure the cuff is deflated, then pull out the tube three to four centimeters

(D) Gently pull the tube three to four inches out, ensuring the cuff is inflated

(5) You have been instructed by medical control to help a patient who has a metered-dose inhaler. What must you ensure before you can begin to help the patient?

(A) The patient is not choking

(B) The medication is right for the patient and has not expired

(C) The inhaler does not have a leak

(D) There is more of the medication in stock at the hospital

(6) What is 'spontaneous pneumothorax'?

(A) Its cause is an impact to the chest, penetrating the patient's lung

(B) It only affects patients who have COPD

(C) It's a sudden buildup of air within the patient's pleural space

(D) It is not as prevalent in men as it is in women

(7) What would you consider a suitable intervention to treat an apneic person?

(A) Oropharyngeal airway

(B) Intubation

(C) BVM Mask

(D) All of the above choices

(8) What kind of injury leads to paradoxical motion affecting a person's chest?

(A) Clavicle break

(B) Hemopneumothorax

(C) Pneumothorax

(D) Flail chest

(9) Often, cardiac arrest in children is the result of:

(A) Hypovolemia.

(B) Compromised respiratory function

(C) Rhythm that is irregular

(D) Chest trauma

(10)   When carrying out artificial ventilation using a bag-valve-mask to help patients whom you consider to have no trauma, you should first:

(A) Use both your hands to fix the mask correctly on the patient's face

(B) Put the patient's head in a 'sniffing' posture that is hyper-extended

(C) Insert an airway adjunct as you choose the appropriate size of mask

(D) Have an assistant squeeze the mask bag until the patient's chest rises

(11)   If a 70-year-old patient whose complaint is being short of breath has had emphysema in the past, what should you do?

(A) Avoid giving oxygen so you do not terminate the present hypoxic drive

(B) Avoid giving oxygen because such patients hardly respond to it

(C) Provide oxygen since often, hypoxic drive does not have an impact

(D) Avoid giving oxygen since such patients end up apneic after receiving oxygen at a high flow

(12)   Utilizing a rigid suction catheter when treating infants and young children risks stimulation of the back of the throat, which may:

(A) Lead to differences in the rhythm of the heart

(B) Become ineffective during suctioning

(C) Cause instant vomiting

(D) Lead to the patient's tongue entering the air passage

(13)   If your 35-year-old patient cannot breathe and you cannot get the airway open using either the jaw thrust or suctioning, what should you do?

(A) Begin mouth-to-mask ventilation

(B) Use the head tilt-chin lift technique

(C) Begin ventilation using a bag-valve-mask

(D) Create an airway via a tracheostomy

(14)   Of the options given below about insufficient breathing, which is correct?

(A) Breathing that is extra fast, or extra slow might be an indication of insufficient breathing

(B) Insufficient breathing is not as common in young children as it is in more elderly adults

(C) Breathing with extra effort is normal and has no association with insufficient breathing

(D) When a patient breathes extra deeply or extra shallowly, it is a move to compensate for abnormal rate of respiration

(15)   The structure that bars food as well as liquids from getting into a person's trachea at the time of swallowing is:

(A) The larynx

(B) The cricoid cartilage

(C) The epiglottis

(D) The diaphragm

(16)   What action should you take if you have a patient with epistaxis?

(A) No treatment is available to cure epistaxis

(B) Use gauze to fill that location

(C) Begin pinching the patient's nostrils while he or she keeps leaning forward

(D) Begin pinching the patient's nostrils while he or she tilts the head back

(17)   What signs & symptoms indicate the patient is in shock?

(A) Increase in heart rate and respirations as well as hypotension

(B) Decrease in heart rate, increase in respirations as well as hypotension

(C) Increase in heart rate, decrease in respirations as well as hypertension

(D) Decrease in heart rate, increase in respirations as well as hypertension

(18)   Your patient is a 22-year-old man with an object lodged in the chest somewhere on the right and beneath his shoulder. You begin by confirming that object has not blocked the airway. What should you do next?

(A) Push out that object by the same route it penetrated

(B) Pull out that object by the same route it penetrated

(C) Break the object near the patient so as to ensure bleeding is under control and then transport that patient

(D) Stabilize the object in one place and then control bleeding before transporting the patient

(19)   When you see a patient whose injury comprises overstretched, torn ligaments, what do you consider those injuries to be?

(A) Fracture

(B) Sprain

(C) Strain

(D) Dislocation

(20)   If you think a patient has fractured the talus bone, what is the most suitable treatment you would recommend?

(A) Application of a traction splint, then heat, followed by elevation of the leg

(B) Application of a traction splint, then ice, followed by elevation of the arm

(C) Splinting of the patient's ankle, application of ice, followed by elevation

(D) Splinting of the patient's foot, application of heat, followed by elevation

(21) You have a patient with an injury at the back of the head. Which specific part of his brain is most likely to be affected?

(A) Parietal

(B) Occipital

(C) Temporal

(D) Frontal

(22) Your 33-year-old male patient has a big laceration on his abdomen, with his abdominal organs protruding out of that opening. What is this kind of injury called?

(A) Evisceration

(B) Protrusion

(C) Avulsion

(D) Contusion

(23) The most suitable means of handling an amputated extremity is:

(A) Packing it in ice

(B) Wrapping it in plastic and placing it on ice

(C) Wrapping it in a sterilized dressing and then keeping it cool using ice

(D) Placing it in a container and filling it with saline solution

(24) If, during transportation of a trauma patient, you observe he is becoming worse, what is the best thing to do?
(A) Stop the ambulance and start CPR

(B) Ask your colleague to drive the ambulance faster so as to reach the hospital as soon as possible

(C) Reassess the patient

(D) Call medical control

(25)   When transporting a patient who is unconscious, you should assess vital signs:

(A) Every 5 minutes

(B) Every 2-3 minutes

(C) Every 10 minutes

(D) Every 15 minutes

(26)   The mnemonic used to determine consciousness level is:

(A) SAMPLE

(B) AVPU

(C) ABC

(D) OPQRST

(27)   You have been called because a male, 16 years of age, has fallen from around 15 feet. You should consider the call:

(A) A non-traumatic emergency

(B) An emergency that is traumatic and which requires the person to be airlifted to the closest Level 1 trauma center

(C) An injury mechanism that is significant

(D) An injury mechanism that is not significant

(28)   If a child below eight years of age fell a distance more than _____, the injury mechanism would certainly be significant.

(A) The patient's height

(B) 5 feet

(C) Twice the height of the patient

(D) 10 feet

(29)   When you arrive at a motor accident scene and notice a man whom a car has hit has clear fluid leaking out of his ear, you conclude the fluid is cerebral spinal. You therefore think the patient has likely suffered:

(A) A serious injury to the head

(B) A cervical spine injury

(C) A basilar skull fracture

(D) A rupture to the eardrum

(30)   When assessing a patient's lower extremities, PMS refers to:

(A) Pulse, motor sensation, severity

(B) Pedial, motion, sensation

(C) Pulse, motor function, sensation

(D) Pain, motion, severity

(31)   When you find a 32-year-old man with complaints of pain in the abdomen as well as weakness, you assess him, and he tells you he also has Addison's disease from the use of steroids when he was a teenager. You do not find any conditions that are a threat to his life as far as his airway, breathing and circulation are concerned.

Specifically, where vital signs are concerned, pulse is 110 bpm; respiration is 16 every minute; blood pressure is 110/72 mmHg while SpO2 is 98 percent gauged against room air. Considering the medical history of the patient, your best option is:

(A) To administer activated charcoal

(B) To give oral glucose

(C) To get in touch with ALS

(D) To assess the level of blood glucose

(32)   The most common cause of anaphylaxis is:

(A) Bee stings

(B) Treatment using penicillin

(C) Treatment using aspirin

(D) Fungi and molds

(33)   In the course of planning a seminar that is part of continuing education in conjunction with the medical director, it is decided there is a need to address emergencies of a behavioral nature. The medical director would like to know how you define 'normal' behavior. What is your response?

(A) Behavior considered normal by the person being monitored

(B) Conduct or activity by a person which someone else can observe

(C) Behavior that is acceptable to society

(D) Behavior that is not hurting anyone

(34)   Your patient is a 52-year-old woman whom neighbors found behaving oddly. She seems fatigued as well as confused, and her speech is slurred. You note she is able to breathe on her own and you can feel her pulse. Her skin is not only cool but mottled. When you take her vital, you note that her pulse is 68 bpm and respirations 14 every minute. Her blood pressure is 108/60 mmHg while her temperature is 92.7°F. You find no trauma signs. She has prescriptions for some medications in the house, namely Verapamil and Digoxin, as well as Synthroid and also nitroglycerin. Nobody knows about her possible allergies. In the meantime, the apartment she is in has a temperature of 55°F. Considering all those findings, which of the conditions listed below is most probable to have led to this patient's health condition?

(A) Hypothyroidism

(B) Atrial fibrillation

(C) Hypertension

(D) Seizure

(35)   A patient who has peptic ulcers is treated with medications like:

(A) Non-steroidal anti-inflammatories

(B) Aspirin

(C) Calcium channel blockers

(D) Antibiotics

(36)   A 17-year-old teenager has all of a sudden begun to be short of breath, and as you assess him, you learn he has Marfan's syndrome. You also observe the sounds from the lungs, on the left of the chest, have diminished and the patient is dyspneic. What, in your view, is the most likely reason the patient is short of breath?

(A) Congenital lung disease

(B) Pulmonary embolism

(C) Spontaneous pneumothorax

(D) Pneumonia

(37)   Insulin has a physiological role in enhancing how well the cells utilize glucose. What happens to someone whose insulin level is low?

(A) Glucose remains within the cells without being functional at all

(B) Insulin levels outside the cell are not enough and hence cannot manage to break down available glucose.

(C) Insulin levels within the cell are not enough and hence cannot manage to break down available glucose.

(D) Glucose remains outside the cells, and nothing can break it down.

(38)   The call that has come in requires that you respond to a teenager at a juvenile detention center who, you're told, has just given himself an opiate injection.

Which drug below is in the opiate category?

(A) Ativan

(B) Heroin

(C) Librium

(D) Cocaine

(39)   At a resort on a mountaintop is a patient who complains of suddenly being short of breath and coughing. After assessing the patient, you realize there are basilar crackles in the lungs and the patient is anxious. The patient's vitals indicate heart rate is 136 and respiration is 28, while blood pressure is 176/94 mmHg. What diagnosis would you give this particular patient as assessed in the field?

(A) A case of high altitude pulmonary edema

(B) Start of congestive heart failure

(C) A case of pneumonia

(D) A case of high altitude congestive heart failure

(40)   'Status epilepticus' means a seizure:

(A) Lasts more than five minutes

(B) Is on a single side of the body

(C) Is known to produce apnea.

(D) Is known to start just as another seizure ends, before the affected patient can regain consciousness.

(41)   As you transport a patient with night sweats and fever that is mild, who also has a productive cough, he mentions he has been receiving treatment from the Department of Health for a condition of a respiratory nature. Which is the most appropriate way of transporting the patient to a medical facility?

(A) As comfortably as the patient can be transported

(B) Putting a mask on him or her as well as on the attendant EMT

(C) As calmly and passively as possible

(D) Using the left lateral recumbent position.

(42)   Vital signs indicate your patient has gone into the shock stage described as being 'decompensated.' What are those signs?

(A) Heart rate is 110 and respirations are 24 while blood pressure is 128/90 mmHg
(B) Heart rate is 64 and respirations are 8 while blood pressure is 82/40 mmHg

(C) Heart rate is 92 and respirations are 18 while blood pressure is 124/72 mmHg

(D) Heart rate is 128 and respirations are 26 while blood pressure is 82/62 mmHg

(43)   You have a patient who believes his illness is about to kill him, and so you are not making much headway in trying to get details from him regarding his symptoms. Which technique is acceptable to use as you interview him?

(A) Reiterate any useful information he has provided and then ask for more.

(B) Give the patient reassurance that he is going to be okay

(C) Be stern and instruct the patient to focus as he provides the information you require

(D) Reduce the physical space between him and you and inform him he is likely to become worse if he cannot provide the information you require.

(44)   You have been sent to attend to a 65-year-old man who has brain cancer and is short of breath. What is the most appropriate action to take considering this patient has an order for Do Not Resuscitate (DNR)?

(A) Talk with the patient's family and see if persuasion can work so that you can transport the patient.

(B) Give oxygen to the patient and then transport him to a suitable emergency unit.

(C) Reach out to your medical director regarding the possibility of giving the patient oxygen but not transporting him.

(D) Get in touch with the oncologist who treats the patient to get directions on the most appropriate care you can provide.

(45)   When attending to a patient whose fingers have suffered frostbite, how best can you prepare those fingers for transportation?

(A) Massage the hands including the fingers, working towards restoring blood circulation

(B) Wrap the patient's fingers one by one

(C) Put a heat pack right on the patient's palms.

(D) Submerge the patient's fingers in warm water.

(46)   Which of the choices below does not cause seizures?

(A) Head injury

(B) Epilepsy

(C) Diabetes

(D) Drug withdrawal

(47)   What would be your major concern if you found someone having seizures?

(A) What type of seizure is the patient having?

(B) When was the last seizure?

(C) What is the patient's past medical history?

(D) What is the patency of the airway?

(48)   You have a patient who has had epileptic fits in the past, and this time, according to his family, he has failed to recover as he usually does after having a seizure. The patient suffers another seizure just as you are assessing him. What is the term given to such a condition?

(A) Tonic-clonic

(B) Status epilepticus

(C) Stacked seizures

(D) Repeatius epilepticus

(49)   There is a form of seizure that causes a patient to simply stare into space and not experience massive muscular contractions. What is it called?
(A) Petit mal

(B) Focal motor

(C) Febrile

(D) Grand mal

(50)   As an EMT, it is not uncommon to encounter cases of allergic reaction, and this is not surprising as many people with allergies are bound to find themselves exposed to the nuisance allergens at one time or another. The process of exposing someone to an allergen is termed_____.

(A) Anaphylactic reaction

(B) Allergic reaction

(C) Sensitization

(D) Anaphylaxis

(51)   One of the entry routes below is the most common as far as anaphylactic reaction causes are concerned. Which is it?

(A) Contact

(B) Inhalation

(C) Ingestion

(D) Injection

(52)   Once EMTs arrive at the emergency scene, their initial concern with regards to the patient is:

(A) Will I get stung?

(B) Is the airway swelling and is there effort of a respiratory nature?

(C) What caused the reaction?

(D) Are there hives?

(53)   Anaphylactic shock is a kind of distributive shock, and in this case, the blood vessels are:

(A) Dilated

(B) Leaking

(C) Constricted

(D) Semi-permeable

(54)   Following appropriate control of a patient's airway in an emergency situation, administration of epinephrine should follow. Why is epinephrine preferable?

(A) It speeds up the heart

(B) It dilates the bronchioles

(C) It constricts blood vessels

(D) All of the above

(55)   Syncope is caused by different things. When does a patient experience a syncopal episode?

(A) When going to bed

(B) Upon standing

(C) When waking up in the morning

(D) Any time

(56)   There are different entry routes through which accidental poisoning can happen. Which among those possible routes is most common?

(A) Inhalation

(B) Injection

(C) Ingestion

(D) Absorption

(57)   There are many poisons that adversely affect people, but there are only a handful of antidotes. What, then, can one use as a treatment when there is a case of poisoning, but an antidote is not available?

(A) Poison removal

(B) Limitation of absorption

(C) Symptom treatment

(D) Elimination of the affected organ

(58)   How does poisonous ingestion happen in children?

(A) Mostly by accident

(B) Mostly forcefully given to them

(C) Mostly children do it on purpose

(D) In most cases, it is through children being neglected or abused

(59)   There are people who inhale poison just to get high. What is the term used for such people?

(A) Puffers

(B) Inhalers

(C) Sniffers

(D) Huffers

(60)   Diagnosing food poisoning away from a hospital environment can be difficult because there is a wide range of symptoms associated with food poisoning. It may take quite some time after food poisoning for the affected person to fall ill. Below is a list of ailments that are all foodborne apart from one. Which is it?

(A) Escherichia coli (E. coli)

(B) Salmonella

(C) Encephalitis

(D) Champylobacter

(61)   What is the common pulse for a newborn child?
(A) 140 to 160

(B) 120 to 140

(C) 100 to 120

(D) 80 to 100

(62)   For a child ages 1 to 6, what is the common pulse rate?

(A) 140 to 160

(B) 120 to 140

(C) 100 to 120

(D) 80 to 100

(63)   What is the common pulse rate for a kid over 6 years old?

(A) 140 to 160

(B) 120 to 140

(C) 100 to 120

(D) 80 to 100

(64)   What is the accurate blood flow from the heart through the lungs?

(A) Superior/inferior venae cava through the right atrium to the right ventricle, through the lungs to the left atrium and left ventricle, then finally to the aorta

(B) Through the aorta to the left atrium and left ventricle, then through the lungs to the right atrium and right ventricle, then finally to the inferior/superior venae cava

(C) Superior/inferior venae cava through the right atrium and right ventricle to the aorta, through the lungs to the left atrium and left ventricle

(D) Right atrium and right ventricle through inferior/superior venae cava to the lungs then aorta to the left ventricle and left atrium

(65)   The angina pectoris has a distinct dissimilarity with a myocardial infarction. What is it?

(A) It is impossible to define the difference for an EMT-B

(B) Aching in the angina pectoris steadily lessens

(C) Time-out automatically gets rid of the myocardial infarction

(D) Constant mental and physical stress causes angina pectoris

(66)   You find an 80-year-old male patient experiencing shortness of breath. What is the most unlikely cause of his distress?

(A) Congestive heart failure

(B) Myocardial infarction

(C) Cardiac compromise

(D) URTI

(67)   On the right side of the heart, there is a three-flapped valve. What is the valve?

(A) The tri-valve

(B) The mitral valve

(C) The tricuspid valve

(D) The triluminar valve

(68)   The sole purpose of the mitral valve is?

(A) Stopping the flow of blood back to the left ventricle

(B) Stopping the flow of blood back to the left atrium

(C) Stopping the flow of blood back to the lungs

(D) Stopping the flow of blood between the ventricles

(69)   A clinician finds that his patient is experiencing discomfort in his chest and puts him in a comfortable position. What should the clinician do next to assist the 45-year-old male?

(A) Using an NRB mask, ventilate the patient at 15 liters every minute

(B) Using the bag-valve mask, ventilate the patient at 15 liters every minute

(C) Using the NRB mask, administer the oxygen at 15 liters every minute

(D) Using the nasal cannula, administer the oxygen at 6 liters every minute

(70)   What should you do first when a 62-year-old patient with a history of heart illness complains that he is suffering from chest pains?
(A) Place the AED pads on his chest

(B) Prepare the automated external defibrillator while you administer CPR in the meantime

(C) Request to help the patient with his nitroglycerin if he has not taken it yet

(D) Administer a lot of oxygen after putting the patient in a comfortable position

(71)   Ventricular fibrillation is often from the conversion of which heart rhythm?

(A) Asystole

(B) Ventricular tachycardia

(C) Atrial fibrillation

(D) Atrial tachycardia

(72)   The pain in a cardiac arrest is usually defined as which of these characteristics by the patients?

(A) Paresthesia

(B) The feel of being squeezed and/or crushed

(C) Irregular pains

(D) Not as bad as heartburn

(73)   The following are patients with various signs and symptoms; which indicates cardiac compromise?

(A) An 85-year-old male with a high fever, quick pulse and breathing complications

(B) A 72-year-old female with stiffness in her throat, wheezing and labored breathing

(C) A 53-year-old female experiencing sudden perspiration, dull chest pain and breathing complications

(D) A 51-year-old male with chest discomfort, headache, dizziness and gagging

(74)   Among the four chambers of the heart, which one pumps blood rich in oxygen to the rest of the body?
(A) Right atrium

(B) Right ventricle

(C) Left atrium

(D) Left ventricle

(75)   If you are alone and find yourself in a situation where a 64-year-old woman has collapsed due to a heart attack, what is the next action to take after assessment and administration of two ventilations?

(A) Analyze the heart rhythm with the AED and, if specified, give a shock

(B) Proceed with chest compressions for a period of a minute

(C) Analyze the heart rhythm with the AED and then proceed with chest compressions

(D) Proceed with chest compressions after calling medical control

(76)   Upon arrival at a scene, you discover a patient whose mental status has been altered. After a quick scan, which of these items would help in pointing to the likely cause for his agitated state of mind?

(A) Untidy house with a dirty floor and scattered animal fur

(B) Medications for depression, anxiety and hypertension

(C) Cat feces and dirty clothes

(D) Over the counter (OTC) painkillers

(77)   When a patient isn't responsive to your loud verbal stimuli and you come across these medications—Lipitor and Glucophage—what is the most likely source of the problem?

(A) Elevated cholesterol

(B) Hypertension

(C) Reaction caused by diabetes

(D) Coronary heart disease

(78)   What would be your primary field diagnosis if your neurological evaluation of a patient that is not responding reveals pinpoint pupils ?

(A) Beta-blocker overdose

(B) An overdose of insulin

(C) Aspirin

(D) Narcotics

(79)   With a diabetic patient that gets 4 injections of insulin a day and has 18 breaths each minute, what would be the most likely reason he was found unresponsive, tachycardic and diaphoretic?

(A) Hypoglycemia

(B) Hyperglycemia

(C) Cerebral vascular accident

(D) Hypertensive distress

(80)   A clinician would give 15 grams oral instant glucose to a diabetic patient that is experiencing hypoglycemia, but not if the patient is _____

(A) Awake with blood sugar

(B) Half-awake and able to swallow with a gag reflex

(C) Half-awake without being able to swallow

(D) Awake with an altered state of mind and blood sugar of 80 mg/dl

(81)   Which one of these is the first sign of diabetes in a lot of young patients and is often a fatal complication?

(A) Being hypoglycemic

(B) High blood pressure

(C) Heart illness

(D) Diabetic ketoacidosis (DKA)

(82)   Apart from thirst, acetone on the breath, frequent urination, poor skin turgor, dry skin, altered mental status and confusion, which other indications are involved with diabetic ketoacidosis (DKA)?

(A) A normal state of mind

(B) The appearance of intoxication

(C) Tremors

(D) Diaphoresis

(83)   The more common of the two kinds of CVA is the ischemic stroke. Which of these is the other kind?

(A) Transient ischemic attack (TIA)

(B) Hemorrhagic stroke

(C) Thrombotic stroke

(D) Embolic stroke

(84)   When the diagnosis of a condition is a TIA, the symptoms must resolve within 24 hours _____?

(A) With few minor shortfalls

(B) With few major long living after effects

(C) Without any memory aftereffects

(D) Without any permanent reactions

(85)   Between the Cincinnati Stroke Scale and the Los Angeles Pre-hospital Stroke Screen, which tool uses arm drift as a diagnostic tool in the assessment of a patient with stroke?

(A) None

(B) Cincinnati Stroke Scale

(C) Los Angeles Prehospital Stroke Screen

(D) Both of them

(86)   Symptoms of a stroke are often similar to other various medical problems, and so, in order to prevent administering the wrong treatment, it is mandatory to work through the differences. An example is how hypoglycemia is usually confused for a cerebral vascular accident. How would one rule out the difference?

(A) Examine the pupils

(B) Check blood sugar

(C) Check the grip

(D) Examine the arm drift

(87)   Rapid transport to the stroke center is by far a clinician's preferred method of treatment and assessment for a stroke patient. Which of these presents the perfect timing for this from the beginning of the indications till treatment?

(A) Any period before symptoms are resolved

(B) Three hours

(C) Within the first 24 hours

(D) When a patient has a stroke, there isn't a way to fix it

(88)   Which of these statements about indications of a stroke would make a clinician highly suspicious?

(A) This is the worst headache I have ever had

(B) Behind my right eye there is pain

(C) My head has been throbbing

(D) My head hurts worse with bright light

(89)   Which of these is the medical condition whereby a patient experiences seizure activity or convulsions from time to time?

(A) Postictal state

(B) Tonic-clonic

(C) Focal motor

(D) Epilepsy

(90)   During assessment, which of these highly suggests that a depressed patient is at risk of suicide?

(A) An unsuccessful previous suicide attempt

(B) Packing of treasured belongings

(C) Hostility towards worried family members

(D) A fresh diagnosis of high blood pressure

(91)   When blood is pumped out of the heart through the heart's right ventricle, where does it go?

(A) The aorta first, then to other parts of the body.

(B) Vena cava first, then the left atrium

(C) Pulmonary veins first, then the lungs

(D) Pulmonary arteries first, then the lungs

(92)   According to research, the biggest cause of shocks inappropriately delivered by Automated External Defibrillators (AEDs) is as a result of _____.

(A) Batteries that have not been properly charged

(B) Electrodes that malfunction

(C) Interference with mechanical parts

(D) Human error

(93)   Which of the statements below is correct when it comes to assessing cardiac-compromised patients?

(A) The extent of any cardiac damage done cannot be determined in the field

(B) Many patients who have suffered cardiac pain describe it as moderately severe and localized

(C) Focused history is used to ascertain whether or not to use an AED

(D) Patients should not be asked about use of nitroglycerin or any other drugs

(94)   Which of the statements below is true regarding the heart's left atrium?

(A) Blood is pumped to the lungs from the left atrium

(B) The pulmonary vein delivers blood to the left atrium

(C) Veins from all over the body deliver blood to the left atrium

(D) Blood is pumped to the body from the left atrium

(95)   AED pads are best applied to patients when they

(A) Seem confused and unaware of what is going around them

(B) Are vomiting and have lost consciousness

(C) Are apneic and don't have a pulse

(D) Are having trouble breathing

(96)   What do you call the two chambers on the lower side of the heart?

(A) Ventricles

(B) Bronchi

(C) Orbits

(D) Atriums

(97)   Which valve is located between the heart's right atrium and ventricle?

(A) Aortic valve

(B) Tricuspid valve

(C) Pulmonic valve

(D) Bicuspid valve

(98)   You arrive at the scene with an elderly male patient complaining of extreme chest pains. He has a history of heart problems. In such a scenario, what is the role medical direction plays?

(A) To talk to the patient and keep him calm

(B) To authorize interventions

(C) To talk to and calm the family

(D) It has no purpose

(99)   You arrive at the scene with an elderly male patient complaining of extreme chest pains. He has a history of heart problems. Without more medical direction, what dosage of nitroglycerin should be given at most?

(A) 4 tablets

(B) 3 tablets

(C) 2 tablets

(D) 5 tablets

(100)   You arrive at the scene with an elderly male patient complaining of extreme chest pains and experiencing breathing difficulties. He is overweight and is a high-capacity chain smoker. Which condition is he likely to have?

(A) Coronary artery disease

(B) Ventricular fibrillation

(C) Pulmonary artery

(D) Pulseless electrical activity

(101)   You arrive at the scene with a young male patient who has a rapid pulse. When questioned, the patient says that he was running. With this information, what are your first thoughts?

(A) The patient requires a nitroglycerin tablet

(B) The patient's reaction is normal.

(C) The patient requires an AED

(D) The patient needs to be moved

(102) You arrive at a scene with an elderly female patient whose heart has stopped. After administering one AED shock, she starts breathing, but at only 15 breaths a minute, and the carotid pulse is very strong. What do you do next?

(A) Ask for a non-transport, then leave

(B) Provide additional oxygen via NRB

(C) Use a bag-valve mask to help ventilations

(D) Continue administering AED shocks

(103) You arrive at a scene to find a male patient who is 50 years of age having cardiac problems. What will happen if his heartbeat is too fast or slow?

(A) He may become extremely agitated

(B) He might lose consciousness

(C) He may begin vomiting

(D) He may have seizures

(104) You arrive at a scene to find a female patient who is 53 years of age and experiencing severe chest pains. After getting medical direction, you administer one nitroglycerin tablet. What should you do next?

(A) Give an additional dose of nitroglycerin

(B) Check the patient's blood pressure

(C) Get the patient to stand upright

(D) Make the patient lie supine

(105) You are sent to a male patient who is 50 years of age and experiencing severe chest pains. Which of the following is a contraindication for giving nitroglycerin?

(A) It is approved by medical direction

(B) The patient's systolic BP is above 100

(C) The patient already has an existing prescription

(D) The patient's systolic BP is below 100

(106) You are at the scene where a patient has just fallen from atop a ladder. When caring for the patient, what should not be taken into consideration?
(A) The length of the ladder.

(B) How high the patient was when he fell

(C) What kind of surface he landed on.

(D) The first body part to hit the ground

(107) You arrive at an MVA where there are three patients with visible but minor injuries. Two of the patients refuse treatment, while the third one complains of back and neck pains. What should be your next course of action?

(A) Since all of them have visible injuries and need medical care, you should treat all of them

(B) Treat the patient with neck and back pains once you get the other two patients to sign refusals

(C) Treat the patient with neck and back pains and leave the others

(D) Treat the patient with neck and back pains as your partner gets the other two patients to sign refusals

(108) You have a male patient who is 17 years of age who was found facedown in the swimming pool. Currently, he is still in the pool, being held with his face above the water. He is breathing, with a steady pulse, although he is still unconscious. How should you proceed?

(A) Get in the pool and start giving CPR

(B) Get the patient out of the pool and immobilize him before transporting him

(C) Get in the pool and apply spinal and cervical immobilization

(D) Patiently wait for a team that is well trained in water rescues

(109) When a laceration spurts bright red blood, which kind of injury does it usually point to?

(A) Vein injury

(B) Artery injury

(C) Injury to capillaries

(D) Injury that requires amputation

(110) You have a patient with a laceration on his right leg that has reached the femoral artery. Blood is still soaking past the bandages even though you've made sure there is pressure directly to the wound. What is the best course of action?

(A) A tourniquet should be applied

(B) Elevate the leg

(C) Replace the old bandages with new ones

(D) Look for a pressure point before the injury and apply pressure on it

(111)   In a motor vehicle crash with impact to the front, the driver wasn't restrained, the steering wheel is bent and the windshield is spidered. What type of energy transfer was there?

(A) Low-velocity penetrating trauma

(B) High-velocity penetrating trauma

(C) Decelerating

(D) Blunt

(112)   How would you classify a penetrating missile that is traveling at speeds exceeding 2,000 feet per second?

(A) Low velocity

(B) Medium velocity

(C) High velocity

(D) Decelerating

(113)   A permanent cavity is formed when a projectile contacts the tissues during penetrating trauma. How do temporary cavities develop?

(A) When the projectile twists

(B) By energy scrubbed off from the projectile

(C) As the wadding enters the body

(D) Due to gunpowder that is unspent

(114) _____ often refers to the way a patient was injured.

(A) Mechanism of injuries

(B) Energy transfer

(C) Injury pattern

(D) Mechanics of injuries

(115) What is the first thing you should do when you approach a trauma incident scene?

(A) Clear airways

(B) C-Spine precautions

(C) Isolate body substances

(D) Ensure the scene is safe

(116) When a lot of blood collects under the skin, this is referred to as _____.

(A) An abrasion

(B) A contusion

(C) A hematoma

(D) A common bruise

(117)   You have a trauma patient whose left hand was caught in a conveyor belt in between rollers. It takes you 30 minutes to extricate the hand. During extrication, you observed that there was a delay in capillary refill distal to the injury. After extrication, you observe rapid capillary refill distal mid-palm to the deformity of the injury. There are no lacerations, no visible fractures and slight swelling. You know there are many problems that may occur as a result of crush injuries. Which of the choices below is not a complication of crush injuries?

(A) Compartment syndrome

(B) Compression of tissues

(C) No injury at all

(D) Fractures

(118)   Traumatic events may lead to tissue loss which may be a part of an extremity, a complete extremity or simply soft tissue. What would you call an injury when a patient loses the distal third of their lower extremity?

(A) Extremity exodus

(B) Avulsion

(C) Amplitude

(D) Amputation

(119)   It is important to control bleeding whenever there is damaged tissue that causes bleeding due to a traumatic event. Which steps should you follow to control the bleeding?

(A) Direct pressure, pressure dressing, tourniquet

(B) Direct pressure, digital pressure, elevation, tourniquet

(C) Direct pressure, elevation, tourniquet, digital pressure

(D) Tourniquet, elevation, pressure dressing, direct pressure

(120) You have a trauma patient who is 16 years of age and has what seems to be a femur fracture located mid-shaft. You see a laceration directly above where the fracture is suspected to be, and the bleeding is under control. Which type of fracture could this be?

(A) Greenstick

(B) Comminuted

(C) Closed

(D) Open

(121) On the way to the hospital, a patient is intubated. During the assessment of the tube placement, a wheezing sound is heard from the lungs. What is the most likely cause of this wheezing sound?

A) An inhalation injury affecting the upper air-conducting passages

B) An inhalation injury caused by cardiac asthma

C) An inhalation injury caused by an asthma attack

D) An inhalation injury affecting the lower air-conducting passages

(122) Which step among the following should a paramedic perform last after immobilizing an extreme fracture of the lower right arm?

A) Ensure that the splint has been tightly applied

B) Put the patient's hand in an appropriate functioning position

C) Assess the distal motor presence and sensory plus perfusion

D) Put the extreme part, already immobilized, below heart level

(123) You encounter a female patient who is 24 years of age and has a gunshot wound on her back. The wound where the bullet exited is not visible and the patient is awake although confused. You realize that she has pale skin and is diaphoretic, with cyanosis to her oral mucosa. The sounds of her breath are quite clear and strong.

The patient's blood pressure is 90/78 mm/Hg, heart rate 124 is bpm and respiratory rate is 28 per minute and strenuous. Sinus tachycardia is also noted on a cardiac monitor. What medical problem is likely to be affecting the patient most?

A) Blood pooling in the pleural cavity

B) Pneumothorax as a result of a wound in the chest

C) Cardiac tamponade

D) Laceration of an aorta

(124) You encounter a boy who has just been hit by a baseball on his nose. The nose has been dislocated to the boy's left and has moderate epistaxis. The patient complains of extreme pain affecting his nose, but luckily he is conscious and alert. Which treatment sequence listed below would be the best to manage such a patient?

(A) Pack the nose using gauze for control of the bleeding

(B) Ensure the patient lies horizontally while putting pressure to the nares

(C) Bring the nose into central position while putting pressure to the nares

(D) Ensure that the patient sits upright and leans forward while putting pressure to the nose

(125) You have been called to attend to an elderly female patient who fell and injured her knee. The patient says that she tripped before falling down, hitting her left knee first. She refutes having lost consciousness and having trauma affecting her head. The patient only complains of pains on her femur's distal area. When assessing her, you realize that her femur has been deformed and is also swollen near the knee. You also note that the patient's distal pulse and motor function, as well as sensation, are good. What, according to you, is the best treatment to offer the patient?

A) Secure the patient on a backboard before cushioning her appropriately

B) Use cushioned boarded splints

C) Use traction splinting

D) Inflate the PASG on the patient's legs

(126) Which among the following types of patients is most suitable to be referred for triage to a center that does not deal with trauma?

(A)A 67-year-old patient who was a victim of electrocution by a 220-volt electrical outlet

(B)A 19-year-old teenage male who was involved in a single-car accident which was traveling at 25 miles per hour

(C)A 25-year-old woman who has a one-inch cut on the thigh

(D)A 14-year-old boy who fell 11 feet from a tree and landed back-first

(127) You are informed about a 37-year-old man in your neighborhood who cut his leg as he was working in his backyard. Before you arrive, the patient's wife, who happens to be a nurse, put pressure on the patient's wound after which she let the patient rest in a Trendelenburg position. After assessing the patient, you note that he is receptive to painful impetuses with a feeble carotid pulse and his blood pressure cannot be obtained. You also note that the patient is surrounded by a lot of blood. The wife informs you that it is an arterial wound and occurred between 10 to 15 minutes prior. Apart from oxygen therapy, which other medical treatments would you prioritize giving the patient?

(A)Continue applying pressure directly on the patient's wound as you seek ALS support.

(B)Ensure application of an arterial bandage as you await ALS support

(C)Do not apply an arterial bandage as you await ALS support

(D)Continuously put pressure on the patient's wound as you transport the patient

(128) Among the findings below, which is the most common and earliest where a crush injury is concerned?

(A) Some pain

(B) Weak pulse

(C) Paresthesia

(D) Paralysis

(129) A 26-year-old woman has been rescued from a house which is on fire. She has suffered burns to her arms and chest. The patient says that she has minor pains where she was burned. What would you consider the most appropriate categorization of the patient's burns?

(A) Third-degree burns

(B) Second-degree burns

(C) Partial-thickness burns

(D) First-degree burns

(130) You are informed of a 43-year-old man who engaged in an altercation and got hit in the face and the head by a baseball bat. He is unresponsive. After evaluating the patient, you realize there is instability in his face from the orbit to the mouth. From the information you have gathered, what is the best way to conclusively manage his airway?

(A) Offer immediate assistance to his ventilations using a bag-valve-mask

(B) Intubate the patient orally and assist his ventilations using a bag-valve-mask

(C) Insert an oral passage and assist his ventilations using a bag-valve-mask

(D) Insert a nasal airway and assist his ventilations using a bag-valve-mask

(131) A gray or bluish skin coloration due to oxygen deficiency is referred to as?

(A)Suffocation

(B)Cyanosis

(C)Tinting

(D)None of the above

(132) What are you required to do for a patient whose oxygen saturation drops significantly after a few breaths of mouth-to-mouth resuscitation by use of an Ambu-bag that has been connected to 100 percent oxygen?

(A)Heighten the respiration rate

(B)Change the patient's head position

(C) Change the mask seal

(D)Remove the oral airway from the patient's mouth.

(133) What is the right amount of air required for injection into the cuff of an endotracheal tube?

(A)1 cc

(B)25 cc

(C)10 cc

(D)100 cc

(134) What is the space between the epiglottis and tongue base referred to as?

(A) Tonsils

(B) Cricoid

(C) Larynx

(D) Vallecula

(135) A strange vocalization, difficult breathing and gasping are all characteristics of which condition?

(A) Agonal breaths

(B) Stridor

(C) Obstructed airway

(D) Wheezing

(136) What is the longest time an intubation attempt can take?

(A) 10 seconds

(B) 30 seconds

(C) 1 minute

(D) 10 minutes

(137) A sound that is high pitched as a result of a turbulent flow of air in the upper airway is characteristic of which condition? It can be expiratory, inspiratory or there during expiration and inspiration.

(A) Respiratory arrest

(B) Wheezing

(C) Stridor

(D) Asthma

(138) The condition where one is unable to move sufficient air as required for perfusion is known as _____.

(A) Respiratory arrest

(B) Respiratory failure

(C) Cardiac failure

(D) Pleurisy

(139) Which one of the following is the wrong technique for confirmation of the correct placement of the endotracheal tube?

(A) Silent epigastrium auscultation.

(B) Visualization of the chest rise and fall.

(C) An equal and clear bilateral breath sound on chest auscultation.

(D) Using commercial carbon dioxide devices.

(140) The tubes that carry air to and from the lungs are referred to as _____.

(A) Bronchi

(B) Larynx

(C) Diaphragm

(D) Ronchi

(141) Stomach expansion due to excess ventilation pressure that causes the extra air to enter the stomach as opposed to the lungs is referred to as what?

(A) Inflation

(B) Gastric distention

(C) Gastric bypass

(D) Evisceration

(142) Which sign listed below is not an indication of breathing adequately?

(A) Inhalation and exhalation through the mouth and nose

(B) Identical expansion of the right and left sides of the chest

(C) Breathing that has been limited to the muscles of the abdomen

(D) Lack of gray/blue coloration of the skin

(143) Observing a patient's _____ can help in detecting whether the patient is suffering from cyanosis.

(A) Tongue

(B) Earlobes

(C) Nail beds

(D) All the above

(144) A nasal and oral airway should:

(A) Be well cleaned in preparation for the next use

(B) Be inserted in patients who have been injured critically

(C) Be useful in preventing the tongue from causing an airway blockage

(D) Be used in preventing suctioning

(145) Name the medication that increases breathing effectiveness and opens bronchioles in patients suffering from shortness of breath.

(A) Bronchodilators

(B) Bronchoconstrictors

(C) Anti-inflammatory

(D) Pneumo-dilator

(146) You have a male patient who is 52 years old. He is suffering from dull chest pain. After assessment, you realize that his skin is clammy, cool and pale despite the fact that he is oriented and alert. What do you do next?

(A) Obtain a blood sample

(B) Apply the AED

(C) Supplement with oxygen

(D) Give him nitroglycerin

(147)   Cardiac compromise refers to:

(A) An angina attack

(B) Heart attack

(C) When the heart fails

(D) Any problem associated with the heart

(148)   What do AEDs treat in patients?

(A) Ventricular fibrillation

(B) Asystole

(C) Pulseless electrical activity

(D) Acute myocardial infarction

(149)   The heart rate of a 0- to 3-month-old-baby is said to be normal at?

(A) 140 to 160

(B) 120 to 140

(C) 100 to 120

(D) 80 to 100

(150)   What is the name of the valve that has two flaps and is on the left of the heart?

(A) Bivalve

(B) Aortic valve

(C) Bicuspid valve

(D) Pulmonary valve

(151)   There are three main components that make up the vascular system. Which one is not one of these components?

(A) Heart

(B) Blood vessels

(C) Myoglobin

(D) Blood

(152)   Starting from outside, which layers cover the heart?

(A) Pericardium, endocardium, epicardium

(B) Myocardium, epicardium, endocardium

(C) Epicardium, myocardium, endocardium

(D) Endocardium, myocardium, epicardium

(153)   From the complaints below, which describes chest pain that is caused by cardiac complications?

(A) Stabbing pains that are sharp and whose location can be identified by a finger

(B) Bricks that weigh a ton on the chest

(C) A feeling like being tickled

(D) Pain like a dull toothache with nagging discomfort

(154) Name the artery that carries blood that does not have oxygen and the vein that carries blood that has oxygen.

(A) Pulmonary, aorta

(B) Pulmonary, inferior vena cava

(C) Pulmonary, pulmonary

(D) Aorta, superior vena cava

(155) Which of these aren't components of blood that cause clotting?

(A) Platelets

(B) Plaque

(C) Thrombin

(D) Fibrin

(156) You have been dispatched to a female patient's residence. She is 46 years old and is suffering from diarrhea, nausea, abdominal cramping and vomiting. She says that she fell ill a short time after eating cheesecake. She is intolerant to lactose. Her BP test shows 136/88. Pulse is 94 bpm while the rate of respiration is 18 breaths in a minute. Before your arrival, she vomited twice. Give your diagnosis.

(A) GERD.

(B) Diverticulitis

(C) Peptic ulcer disease.

(D) Acute gastroenteritis

(157)   You have a male patient who is 32 years old. He complains of a severe crushing feeling at the center of the chest and difficulty in breathing which started when he was mowing the lawn three quarters of an hour before your arrival. The pain stimuli seems to be working on him. At the moment, he has adequate ventilation, pulse is 95 percent, and his skin is cool, diaphoretic and pale. Your first action would be to give:

(A) 12 to 15 liters of oxygen

(B) 325 mg aspirin

(C) 4 to 6 liters of oxygen

(D) Sublingual nitroglycerin

(158)   Your patient, who is 76 years old, has swelling in the legs and is in a wheelchair. After assessment, it is confirmed that she has edema. You do a bilateral pulse palpitation. The skin is pink, dry and warm. The lungs are clear. Which of the following conditions could she be suffering from?

(A) Deep vein thrombosis

(B) Bilateral acute arterial occlusion

(C) Atherosclerosis

(D) Chronic CHF

(159) Your patient is 49 years old and is complaining of pain between the shoulder blades and radiating to the lower back. The pain is constant and started 10 minutes before you arrived, while the patient was eating. Told to rate the pain, the patient gives it a 10/10 and describes it as sharp and tearing. The BP is 130/76 and 78/48 in the right and left arms respectively. Pulse is 98 bpm and is regular while the rate of respiration is 20 per min and is non-labored. Which of the following conditions would you suspect?

(A) Myocardial infarction

(B) Angina pectoris

(C) Aortic dissection

(D) Congestive heart failure

(160) Death in America is mostly caused by?

(A) Coronary heart disease

(B) Chronic obstructive airway disease

(C) Cancer

(D) Traumatic injuries

(161) The highest running speed of a nasal cannula should be:

(A) 2 lpm

(B) 8 lpm

(C) 12 lpm

(D) 6 lpm

(162)   The description below refers to which device?

It's intended to ease a patient's sightless intubation and comprises cuffed double-lumen tube whose one end is blind. The cuff's rise permits this device to carry out a role as the endotracheal tube and ends the esophagus, permitting air passage as well as avoiding gastric reflux substances.

(A) Nasal gastric tube

(B) Dual lumen air passage

(C) Endotracheal tube

(D) Non-rebreather

(163)   To provide oxygen therapy at "100 percent," what should be the flow rate's reading?

(A) 12–15 LPM

(B) 100 LPM

(C) 20–24 LPM

(D) 2–6 LPM

(164)   A man falls from a ladder, which leads to him suffering respiratory pain. Which air passage tactic could you use?

(A) Tilting of the head-lifting of the chin

(B) Intubation

(C) Bite block

(D) Jaw thrust

(165)   From the terminologies listed below, please identify which one refers to a device which transports a certain medicine quantity towards the lungs as a small burst of aerosolized medication which is gasped down by patients.

(A) Nebulizer

(B) Aero chamber

(C) Metered-dose inhaler

(D) Albuterol infuser

(166)   The air passage comprises high as well as low airways. The higher airway begins from the mouth and nares, which is concluded at _____?

(A) The thyroid cartilage

(B) The epiglottis

(C) The cricoid cartilage

(D) The vocal cords

(167)   The most common obstruction of the airway is the tongue, which drops to the back and occludes the _____?

(A) Larynx

(B) Trachea

(C) Nasopharynx

(D) Pharynx

(168) A person's airway on the lower side has its end where the alveoli are found, and that is where exchange of gases occurs. Oxygen enters the hemoglobin through the semi-permeable membrane. The place where this occurs is _____.

(168)

(A) Capillary bed

(B) Bronchioles

(C) Blood capillaries

(D) Veinules

(169) The diaphragm reduces, moving _____ in order to generate force at the thorax or chest cavity. This increases the thorax's volume, letting air rush inside the lungs.

(A) Up direction

(B) Externally

(C) Down direction

(D) Diaphragm doesn't make movements; wall of the chest enlarges.

(170) The diaphragm recovers its domed figure when it relaxes. The act brings about a rise in thoracic force that pushes the air from the person's lungs. Force at the thorax is required to increase over _____ pressure in order to ensure air is pushed from the lungs.

(A) Transthoracic

(B) Atmospheric

(C) Transabdominal

(D) Respiratory

(171)   What ventilation technique has higher chances of yielding the minimal tidal volume?

(A) One-person bag-valve-mask

(B) Two-person bag-valve-mask

(C) Flow-restricted oxygen-powered ventilatory device

(D) Mouth-to-mask

(172)   To help with intubation, a paramedic could make use of Sellick's maneuver, a procedure where the cartilage being compressed is the _____.

(A) Cricoid cartilage

(B) Aryepiglottic cartilage

(C) Thyroid cartilage

(D) Hyoid cartilage

(173)   You are transporting an elderly man experiencing respiratory distress and who also has been diagnosed in the past with COPD.

The unwell male has very light breathing with slight chest-wall movement as well as minor wheezing at the higher lung fields. Given these symptoms, your arterial CO2 intensities expectations would be _____.

(A) Insufficient info to conclude

(B) Ordinary

(C) Dropped

(D) Raised

(174)   You are transporting an ailing 48-year-old man from one medical facility to another. From the past record, you notice the man fell while working which led to his hip fracture as well as a head injury. At the moment, the man is going through labored inhalation of 30 per minute which has gradually become worse over the past day. The heart's frequency is 104, while blood pressure is 98/70. On listening, you notice diffuse rales on auscultation. The patient refutes pain experiences apart from the ones in relation to falling not so long ago. The greatest source of his respiratory pain would be?

(A) Cardiogenic shock

(B) Clogged heart loss

(C) Acute bronchitis

(D) Mature person's respiratory pain syndrome

(175)   The best method when it comes to administering ventilations to a patient who is apneic is _____.

(A) Two-person bag-valve-mask.

(B) FROPVD

(C) One individual bag-valve-mask.

(D) CPR

(176)   You arrive at an emergency scene and notice it seems like a domestic argument is going on regarding molestation of a child. You want to ask a child who is 5 years old about habits of elimination. Identify the word that would be most appropriate to use.

(A) Pee-pee
(B) Micturation
(C) Urination
(D) Deltrusion

(177) If you are put in charge of designing a deployment plan for ambulances within the EMS system in your own community, and you are aiming at minimizing response time even as you utilize every available resource in the most efficient, cost-effective manner possible, which piece of information from the choices provided below would you consider of utmost value?

(A) Where the most recent ambulance collision took place

(B) The time and location of the previous five years' calls

(C) The average of the population's age

(D) The neighborhood's economic status and demographics

(178) Which statement associated with continuous education does the public most value?

(A) It indicates EMTs are sincere about giving their best

(B) It meets guidelines laid out for any EMTs to fulfill state recertification

(C) It allows EMTs to maintain certification at the National Registry.

(D) It serves as a chance for EMTs to learn new and changing skills as well as about medications.

(179) You are called to an industrial compound in a neighborhood where an incident is linked to potentially hazardous material. You are immediately informed that the number of employees affected is around 30 and also that there are many whom fumes have affected.

The team responsible for dealing with hazardous materials has been sent out, and it is estimated it will arrive at the emergency scene 20 minutes after the accident.

On reaching the scene, you find a worker at the entrance who informs you of the apparent contamination source, which is a huge white tank. There is a symbol, "NFPA 704" with several colors, and within a bluish diamond '4' is written. In a red diamond, '1' is written, and another diamond that is yellow. A white diamond contains no number.

A crowd approaches and informs you they have been exposed to some fluid that leaked from the huge tank. What action should you immediately take?
(A) Start triage for those patients, ensuring you obtain their vital signs in order to establish a baseline

(B) Mix a weak bleach solution and instruct the affected workers to use it in decontaminating the exposed areas of their skin

(C) Instruct those patients to get rid of their clothes and then rinse them using water

(D) Instruct those patients to stay in one place until the team specializing in dealing with hazardous material arrives

(180) An EMT would benefit most from stress management following a critical incident such as the:

(A) Demise of a four-year-old boy following a bad fall

(B) Demise of a male, 30 years of age, involved in an accident while driving under the influence of alcohol

(C) Demise of a 43-year-old woman following an explosion

(D) Demise of an 82-year-old woman from suicide

(181) If you release a patient's information to a newspaper and the patient considers that slander and sues you, what particular area of the statute could that patient's suit be based on?

(A) Criminal

(B) Constitutional

(C) Tort

(D) Federal

(182) What would you say is the importance of EMTs and other paramedics completing a checklist of equipment as every shift begins?

(A) Such a list is required by most medical insurance companies for use in liability coverage

(B) Completing such a list minimizes liability risk linked to provision of pre-hospital medical care

(C) Such a checklist is demanded by the country's Occupational Safety & Health Administration

(D) The country's Health & Human department mandates such completion

(183) You are your service's quality assurance committee's head. As you carry out a review of patient health-care reports before handing them in to your medical director, you notice a narrative indicating the patient had no bowel movements and also that he had had pain in the abdomen for a period of around three weeks. It is also documented that the patient had a fever that morning and took Tylenol tablets before experiencing nausea. What would be your advice to the relevant paramedic based on the report?

(A) Ensure EMT-B does comprehensive documentation

(B) Create abbreviations to represent any of the words whose spelling you are not sure of

(C) Document only the things you can spell correctly

(D) Make use of a dictionary in confirming the spelling of words you are unsure of before doing your documenting.

(184) The rules governing the behavior of EMT professionals are:

(A) Morals

(B) Ethics

(C) Various standards

(D) Code of conduct

(185) Soon after arriving at a residence you hear three sounds like gunshots. What immediate action should you take?

(A) Inform dispatch about the situation

(B) Inform the police

(C) Just enter the residence since you cannot see a shooter anywhere

(D) Abandon the emergency scene until the police have secured it.

(186) You arrive at a scene where a vehicle has hit a tree and the driver is slumped unconscious over the car's steering wheel as fire rages, burning the vehicle. You can even see fire in the passenger area. What is your first priority?

(A) Begin by taking care of the safety of bystanders

(B) Begin by taking care of the safety of personnel from the fire department

(C) Immediately rescue the person in the car

(D) Begin by taking care of your own safety and your partner's.

(187) You have just released care of child suspected to be a victim of abuse to the hospital's emergency department. While discussing the situation with the crew from another ambulance, you are overheard by a family member saying the mother of the child is the most likely perpetrator of the abuse. What might you legally be accused of?

(A) Libel

(B) Negligence

(C) Malfeasance

(D) Slander

(188) In the CQI programs, where the abbreviation stands for 'continued quality improvement,' one of the options below is not included in the EMS system. Which is it?

(A) Development and implementation of policies of a disciplinary nature to cater for any kind of variance involving care given by EMTs.

(B) Gathering statistics involving the volume of calls and profiles of patients as well as skills employed

(C) Allowing opportunities in identifying potential medical topics for continuous education involving providers of emergency services.

(D) Creating an internal checks & balances system, which can ensure quality health care is provided and that weaknesses in the system are pinpointed

(189) As you compile a report pertaining to a patient, you note that your patient was intoxicated and deliberately uncooperative. Such statements of a subjective nature can expose you to a legal suit involving:

(A) Malfeasance

(B) Libel

(C) Res ipsa loquitur

(D) Slander

(190)   The agency charged with regulation of EMS radio communications is:

(A) The Federal Communications Commission (FCC)

(B) The National Highway Traffic Safety Administration (NHTSA)

(C) The National Association of Emergency Medical Technicians (NAEMT)

(D) Federal Emergency Management Agency (FEMA)

(191)   A young girl, nine years of age, has been hit by a vehicle and the police cannot get ahold of her parents. Once dispatched to the scene, what will enable you to offer her treatment?

(A) Consent that is expressed

(B) Consent that is revoked

(C) Consent that is implied

(D) Consent that is informed

(192)   What would be the correct action to take at '123 Somewhere Road' where there is a woman who has been injured, but the door is opened by a man who informs you that it is not your business and you should leave?

(A) Go back to your ambulance and inform dispatch about the woman turning down care

(B) Reason with the man, explaining to him that the patient may be in need of medical care

(C) Return to your ambulance and, after you drive a safe distance, call for help from the police

(D) Move forcefully past the person who opened the door and offer help to the patient

(193) When an EMT treats a patient who has refused the treatment, which crime has he/she committed?

(A) Slander

(B) Battery

(C) Medical malpractice

(D) Kidnapping

(194) Protecting oneself and the patient from transferring bodily fluids is referred to as _____.

(A) Universal precautions

(B) Body substance isolation

(C) Wearing gloves

(D) Being safe

(195) People who offer help to the injured are protected from legal suits by which law?

(A) Such a law does not exist.

(B) EMT Registration

(C) Good Samaritan law

(D) Duty to act

(196) Name the areas where ambulances face the most risks of collision.
(A) While leaving the bay

(B) When driving on the freeway

(C) At an intersection

(D) Arriving at the emergency site

(197) Headlights aren't deemed important 'emergency warning lights.' When should they be used?

(A)When moving along the road

(B)Returning from a call

(C)While responding to an emergency call

(D)During transport to the hospital

(198) When responding to incidents involving hazardous materials, where are EMTs supposed to approach a scene from?

(A)Upwind, uphill or upriver

(B)Upwind, uphill or downriver

(C)Downwind, downhill or downriver

(D)Downwind, over a hill or downriver

(199) Name the zone where an EMS is supposed to be set in a hazardous material incident.

(A)Hot zone

(B)Lukewarm zone

(C)Warm zone

(D)Cold zone

(200) When is it considered all right to transport patients directly from hot zones without having to undergo decontamination?

(A)When patients are in need of life-saving actions

(B)At no one time because, regardless of a patient's sickness, he/she must undergo decontamination

(C)Whenever an EMS commander finds it to be all right

(D)When patients have only suffered minor exposure

(201) After calling 'air medical services' for a victim who has been involved in an accident, the aircraft gets in touch with you five minutes after takeoff asking for information about the landing zone. What should not be left out in the safety brief?

(A) Obstructions occurring overhead

(B) The type of area and surface (i.e., gravel, a field, etc.)

(C) Powerful electricity lines a quarter mile away from the landing zone

(D) All of the above.

(202) What patient would be the best fit for air transportation from the scene?

(A) A male patient, 55 years old, who has a fracture on the lower leg caused by stepping into a construction site hole

(B) A male patient, 55 years old, who has been stung by bees multiple times but is not complaining of hives, difficulty swallowing or shortness of breath

(C) A male patient, 55 years old, who fell while standing and has a complaint of swelling of the ankle and a bruise on the left elbow

(D) A male, 55 years old, who has been involved in an accident caused by his speeding motorcycle crashing into a cement highway barrier

(203) On arrival at the facility where patients are received, you have to transfer care to emergency department staff. This task is handled by the duty nurse, using a report indicating the medical history, an assessment of the patient's complaints and interventions in order to allow for_____?

(A) Care to continue

(B) Prime directive

(C) Quantum of care

(D) Great care transfer

(204) The EMTs in charge inform dispatch of arrival at an accident scene involving several cars and explain their findings. "We are at the scene of an accident involving three cars. The patients are not in the cars but are walking around." This information is referred to as?

(A) Scene arrival notification

(B) Report to receiving facility

(C) Scene size-up

(D) Dispatch information

(205) On arrival at a scene, which action is of utmost importance by the EMT?

(A) Positioning oneself to quickly leave the squad

(B) Positioning the squad to make access easy

(C) Squad positioning for scene protection

(D) Squad positioning some miles away and then walking to the scene

(206) To willfully leave a patient who is in need of care without a signed or verbal refusal of care is _____?

(A) Permitted in cases when a patient has been rude or abusive

(B) Considered abandonment

(C) Considered refusal that is implied

(D) Going against medical advice

(207) Which statement about disposable gloves is correct?

(A) When you want to remove your gloves, grasp their ends using the fingers of your other hand and pull

(B) If you want to suction or ventilate a patient using a bag-valve-mask, wearing gloves is unnecessary

(C) You can protect yourself and your patient from disease transmission by wearing gloves

(D) All you need is a single pair of gloves irrespective of the number of patients you are handling

(208) EMTs wear 'High Efficiency Particulate Air' respirators (HEPA) whenever the patients they engage with have:

(A) Hepatitis B

(B) Tuberculosis

(C) HIV or AIDS

(D) Open wounds

(209) In which of the following situations should you call for immediate assistance?

(A) When you have two gunshot-wound patients to care for and they are in critical condition

(B) When you have a 25-year-old patient actively in labor

(C) When you have a pediatric patient who has a fever and has briefly had a seizure

(D) When a patient with a cervical spine injury has required the services of your partner

(210) As you near a scene with potentially hazardous material, one way of identifying hazards is:
(A) Personally carrying out a thorough investigation of that scene

(B) Conducting an interview with victims as well as bystanders

(C) Using binoculars to scan from a safe distance

(D) Helping the police during their search

(211) Once medical direction issues orders, the very first thing you should do is:
(A) Immediately act on those orders

(B) Repeat those orders to confirm what you heard

(C) Seek clarification for whatever you are not sure you understood

(D) Document those orders by including them in your report.

(212) Which option shows appropriate communication involving a patient?

(A) When the patient is 12 years old: "Would you like to hold Mommy's hands as I put a bandage on your wound?"

(B) When in conversation with a 27-year-old male: "Just stand up. You are only intoxicated and have no injuries whatsoever."

(C) When the patient is a 75-year-old female: "Madam, in our opinion you need to be checked at the hospital just to ensure you are fine. Would you mind coming with us?"

(D) When the patient is four years old: "You are likely to have a fractured femur. We shall ensure you are well stabilized before we take you to the hospital for surgery."

(213) What procedure would you consider correct in handling a used adjunct airway?
(A) Dispose of it by throwing it into a biohazard container.

(B) Clean the airway using alcohol before drying it properly

(C) Disinfect it using water mixed with bleach

(D) Sterilize it using an autoclave or water that is boiling hot.

(214) As for the right of a patient to reject care, the correct statement is:
(A) Any child old enough to comprehend danger can be considered old enough to reject care as well as transport

(B) A mature patient with a sound mind who is also able to understand consequences has the right to reject treatment

(C) Nobody has the right to give authority for another to be treated or transported, the patient's age notwithstanding

(D) As an EMT you need to leave the scene as soon as the patient expresses an unwillingness to be treated or given emergency care

(215) The importance of incident management systems is because they:

(A) Create an explicit command chain in case of legal issues
(B) Provide a way to evaluate how EMS systems respond to events
(C) Are an orderly communication method that can help in making decisions
(D) Provide a first responders' program for training

(216) When it comes to patient/EMT confidentiality, it is correct that:

(A) Patients in some public areas do not enjoy confidentiality rights

(B) Minors have no confidentiality rights

(C) Any patient signing a statement to release information of a confidential nature effectively relinquishes other privacy rights

(D) It is necessary for your patient to sign a written release to enable disclosure of confidential information. Otherwise, you cannot release it

(217) In order for handwashing to be effective, it should take a minimum of:

(A) 1 to 2 minutes
(B) 45 to 50 seconds
(C) 25 to 30 seconds
(D) 10 to 15 seconds

(218) You need to put on a mask and eye protection whenever:

(A) You are beginning patient transportation
(B) You are beginning patient suctioning
(C) You are beginning splinting of a closed injury
(D) You are beginning oxygen administration.

(219) Which situation below represents implied consent?

(A) When a 6-year-old patient has a broken arm or leg and you splint it after her mother has given permission

(B) When a patient with cardiac problem requests that you assist him in taking some nitroglycerin

(C) When, on arrival at a car accident scene, you hear the injured driver say: "Please first assist my daughter."

(D) When you offer an unconscious man life support after he was found by strangers

(220) If you have a patient who cannot communicate in English, the best thing to do is:

(A) Do not speak to that patient as you could be misunderstood

(B) Document all actions you perform and have that patient sign the paperwork

(C) Try and contact a person capable of interpreting, either a relative or a bystander

(D) Reject the emergency call and request that the service send a bilingual EMT

Answers & Explanations to NREMT Exam Questions

1. If you reach the site where a woman of advanced age has fallen and injured her ribs, and when you check you find she is breathing rapidly and shallowly, the rate being 40, how can you confirm that this emergency is life-threatening?

The correct answer is: B) There is the risk of her volume per minute diminishing

In the prevailing state, it is possible the patient is not mobilizing sufficient air to penetrate the tissues.

2. EMTs normally use an endotracheal tube:

The correct answer is: C) For insertion inside the patient's trachea

Once inside the patient's trachea, the endotracheal tube separates the trachea and the esophagus, creating a patent airway.

3. 'Sellick's maneuver' is meant for

The correct answer is: A) Reducing vomiting risk

Sellick's maneuver decreases the chances of vomiting as intubation continues, and this is accomplished when the esophagus is directly collapsed. The maneuver also helps in making the patient's vocal cords clearly visible.

4. Once you have the endotracheal tube in place, and as you perform auscultation, you realize the patient's right side has sounds from the lungs but the left does not, or they are minimal. What should be your next move?

The correct answer is: C) Ensure the cuff is deflated, then pull out the tube three to four centimeters

If ever there are audible sounds of the lungs emanating from the right as opposed to the left following intubation, chances are the tube has penetrated the patient's right bronchi. Such a situation happens because the right side has a straighter angle.

5. You have been instructed by medical control to help a patient who has a metered-dose inhaler. What must you ensure before you can begin to help the patient?

(E) The correct answer is: B) The medication is right for the patient and has not expired

Before you can begin helping someone use a metered-dose inhaler, you need to ensure the medication being administered is theirs, and that it has not reached its date of expiration.

6. What is it 'spontaneous pneumothorax'?

(E) The correct answer is: C) It's a sudden buildup of air within the patient's pleural space

It is common to find patients with COPD also developing spontaneous pneumothoraxes. However, the condition could also result from rupturing of particular kinds of blisters within the patient's lungs.

7. What would you consider a suitable intervention to treat an apneic person?

The correct answer is: D) All the above choices

When a person is said to be 'apneic,' it means that person is not taking any breaths; no breathing whatsoever. As such, any of the choices provided are important to try to get the person to resume breathing.

8. What kind of injury leads to paradoxical motion affecting a person's chest?

The correct answer is: D) Flail chest.

A person develops flail chest when there are several ribs adjacent to one another that are broken in different places, in a manner that leaves a section within the person's chest moving independently. That act of moving independently is referred to as 'paradoxical motion.'

9. Often, cardiac arrest in children is the result of :

The correct answer is B) Compromised respiratory function.

Usually when children suffer cardiac arrest, it is because their breathing is insufficient or their respiratory function has been compromised.

10. When carrying out artificial ventilation using a bag-valve-mask to help patients whom you consider to have no trauma, you should first

The correct answer is: B) Put the head of the patient in a 'sniffing' posture that is hyper-extended

As you put the head of the patient in the position described as 'sniffing' and also hyper-extended, you need to keep in mind the sequence in which you can attempt the other emergency moves. If need be, you can insert an adjunct airway, as indicated in C), then use both your hands to fix the mask as represented in A). Finally, have an assistant squeeze the mask bag to ensure the patient's chest rises, as indicated in D).

11. If a 70-year-old patient whose complaint is being short of breath has had emphysema in the past, what should you do?

The correct answer is: C) Provide oxygen since often, hypoxic drive does not have an impact.

It is correct that providing excessive oxygen over long durations could lead to hypoxic drive failure, but it is also a rare eventuality when giving emergency help away from a hospital setup. If the patient is complaining of being short of breath, work towards getting the patient totally oxygenated as opposed to taking a risk just for fear the patient could be hypoxic. In any case, 'EMT Basic' requires ventilation in case the patient suffers respiratory arrest owing to excessive oxygen levels.

12. Utilizing a rigid suction catheter when treating infants and young children risks stimulation of the back of the throat, which may :

The correct answer is: A) Lead to differences in the rhythm of the heart

If a rigid catheter is used when suctioning infants or tiny children, you need to be careful to avoid touching the back of their throat because if that area is stimulated that could lead to bradycardia due to a patient's vagus nerve being stimulated.

13. If your 35-year-old patient cannot breathe and you cannot get the airway open using either the jaw thrust or suctioning, what should you do?

The correct answer is: B) Use the head tilt-chin-lift technique

The reality is that head tilt/chin-lift is normally not given priority when treating trauma patients, and this is because it is known to interfere with the immobilization of the patient's spine as well as its alignment. However, airway opening takes precedence over every other consideration. You just need to make sure you document your every action in the patient's care reports.

14. Of the options given below about insufficient breathing, which is correct?

The correct answer is: A) Breathing that is extra fast, or extra slow might be an indication of insufficient breathing.

If rate of respiration is extra slow or extra fast, this could signify insufficient breathing. A person can suffer distress related to respiration accompanied by myriad medical and trauma issues, and such conditions can affect people of any age. This means choice (B) cannot be correct.

Normally the patient has to put extra work or effort into breathing whenever there is insufficient breathing, in an attempt to compensate. However, this should not be taken to be a signal of normalcy as choice (C) suggests. There are also varied reasons for patients breathing shallowly, and sometimes deeply, and just one of those reasons is compensation for the rate being abnormal; meaning choice (D) cannot be correct.

15. The structure that bars food as well as liquids from getting into a person's trachea at the time of swallowing is:

The correct answer is: C) Epiglottis

The term 'epiglottis' refers to a body structure that is shaped like a leaf, which closes off a person's trachea at the time of swallowing. As for 'larynx,' this is used in reference to a person's voice box, which is the structure that produces vibrations of speech. The 'cricoid cartilage' constitutes the larynx' lower part, while the diaphragm refers to a big muscle which contracts as it initiates inhalation.

16. What action should you take if you have a patient with epistaxis?

The correct answer is: C) Begin pinching the patient's nostrils while he or she keeps leaning forward

Epistaxis simply means nosebleed. If a person's nose is bleeding, tilting the head backwards could lead to aspiration of blood, and then the person will become sick and end up vomiting.

17. What signs & symptoms indicate the patient is in shock?

The correct answer is: A) Increase in heart rate and respirations as well as hypotension

Heightened heart rate and respirations point to the onset of shock, and you may also find the patient pale and cool with clammy skin. Such a patient may also have hypoxia signs. In a later shock stage, the patient's blood pressure might drop.

18. Your patient is a 22-year-old man with an object lodged in the chest somewhere on the right and beneath his shoulder. You begin by confirming that the object has not blocked the airway. What should you do next?

The correct answer is: D) Stabilize the object in one place and then control bleeding before transporting the patient.

Any object that is impaling a patient ought to be removed only if it is obstructing a patient's airway. Otherwise, removal of the object in a pre-hospital setting might lead to bleeding that is not possible to control and that might lead to death. If the object is cut, it could also end up moving around and causing additional injury.

19. When you see a patient whose injury comprises overstretched, torn ligaments, what do you consider those injuries to be?

The correct answer is: B) Sprain

Out in the field, you are expected to handle all the injuries listed in the same manner, but the one described can only be a sprain. A sprain involves injury to ligaments while dislocations affect joints. Fractures are associated with bone injury while strains are related to muscle injuries.

20. If you think a patient has fractured the talus bone, what is the most suitable treatment you would recommend?

The correct answer is: C) Splinting of the patient's ankle, application of ice, followed by elevation

A person's talus bone lies at the top of the foot, within the navicular, tibia, fibula as and calcaneus. In a case like this one, you need to splint the patient's ankle so as to render it immobile, and then ice it in order to decrease the swelling, after which you should elevate the limb.

21. You have a patient with an injury at the back of the head. Which specific part of his brain is most likely to be affected?

The correct answer is: B) Occipital

The rear part of a person's brain is the brain's occipital region, and this is the area of the brain with the greatest likelihood of injury when there is trauma at the back of the head.

22. Your 33-year-old male patient has a big laceration on his abdomen, with his abdominal organs protruding out of that opening. What is this kind of injury called?

The correct answer is: A) Evisceration

'Evisceration' simply means removal of internal organs or their protrusion.

23. The most suitable means of handling an amputated extremity is:

The correct answer is: C) Wrapping it in a sterilized dressing and then keeping it cool using ice

The amputated extremity should be wrapped in a sterile dressing to prevent infection and ice should be used to ensure it remains cool. The bo9dy part should not be placed directly on ice as that could cause frostbite. How well a patient is handled, along with the amputated limb, is critical when it comes to how successful a reattachment is.

24. If, during transportation of a trauma patient, you observe he is becoming worse, what is the best thing to do?

The correct answer is: C) Reassess the patient

When a patient's condition is getting worse, it is always important to reassess.

25. When transporting a patient who is unconscious, you should assess vital signs:

The correct answer is: A) Every 5 minutes

As you transport a patient who is unconscious, it is important that you check their vital signs in intervals of five minutes.

26. The mnemonic used to determine consciousness level is:

The correct answer is: B) AVPU

The mnemonic 'AVPU' represents 'Alert,' response to 'Verbal' stimulus, response to 'Painful' stimulus and 'Unresponsive.'

27. You have been called because a male, 16 years of age, has fallen from around 15 feet high. You should consider the call:

The correct answer is: D) An injury mechanism that is not significant.

A person 16 years old is medically considered an adult, and any adult fall below 20 feet is not considered an injury mechanism with significance.

28. If a child below 8 years old fell a distance more than _____, the injury mechanism would certainly be taken to be significant.

The correct answer is: D) 10 feet

The most suitable answer is 10 feet. Sometimes, though, some children are tall enough to have their double height constituting more than 10 feet. So, ideally, the appropriate answer should be any height 10 feet and above.

29. When you arrive at a motor accident scene and notice a man whom a car has hit has clear fluid leaking out of his ear, you conclude the fluid is cerebral spinal. You, therefore, think the patient has likely suffered:

The correct answer is: A) A serious injury to the head

It is right to say you may have a patient like this one who has a basilar skull fracture, but since it is not possible to establish that while you are out of the hospital setup, your most suitable answer here can only be a serious injury to the head.

30. When assessing a patient's lower extremities, PMS refers to:

The correct answer is: C) Pulse, motor function, sensation

PMS represents 'pulse,' 'motor function' and 'sensation.' It is particularly crucial that you assess the patient for PMS following splinting of an extremity.

31. When you find a 32-year-old man with complaints of pain in the abdomen as well as weakness, you assess him, and he tells you he also has Addison's disease from the use of steroids when he was a teenager. You do not find any conditions that are a threat to his life as far as his airway, breathing and circulation are concerned.

Specifically, where vital signs are concerned, pulse is 110 bpm; respiration is 16 every minute; blood pressure is 110/72 mmHg while SpO2 is 98 percent gauged against room air. Considering the medical history of the patient, your best option is:
The correct answer is: D) To assess the level of blood glucose.

It is crucial to make a point of always checking the level of glucose in the blood whenever you're dealing with a patient who has a problem of adrenal insufficiency.

32. The most common cause of anaphylaxis is:

The correct answer is: B) Treatment using penicillin

In most cases, anaphylaxis is caused by antibiotics, including penicillin. According to data from authorities, there is one allergic reaction out of every 10,000 patients being treated with penicillin, and the rate of related deaths is 500 in a year.

Conversely, cases of people dying from being stung by bees are fewer than 100 annually. The other causes listed are generally rare cases of anaphylactic reactions, so they cannot be taken to be the most common cause.

33. In the course of planning a seminar that is part of continuing education in conjunction with the medical director, it is decided there is a need to address emergencies of a behavioral nature. The medical director would like to know how you define 'normal' behavior. What is your response?

The correct answer is: C) Behavior that is acceptable to the society

Granted, it is not easy to compose a universally acceptable definition of 'normal' behavior, but there is behavior any society considers normal and acceptable from its members. If an individual takes some form of behavior to be normal, but that does not match with what society sees as normal, then overall that form of behavior will be considered abnormal.

A good example is when someone considers clothing optional. Modern society does not consider walking nude in public normal, and so irrespective of what the individual thinks about nudity, being nude in public still remains abnormal behavior. That remains the reality even when the individual's behavior does not cause any discernible harm to anyone. Behavior comprises conduct that is observable, coupled with a person's actions.

34. Your patient is a 52-year-old woman whom neighbors found behaving oddly. She seems fatigued as well as confused, and her speech is slurred. You note she is able to breathe on her own and you can feel her pulse. Her skin is not only cool but mottled. When you take her vital, you note that her pulse is 68 bpm and respirations 14 every minute. Her blood pressure is 108/60 mmHg while her temperature is 92.7°F. You find no trauma signs.

She has prescriptions for some medications in the house, namely Verapamil and Digoxin, as well as Synthroid and also nitroglycerin. Nobody knows about her possible allergies. In the meantime, the apartment she is in has a temperature of 55°F.

Considering all those findings, which of the conditions listed below is the most probable to have led to this patient's health condition?
The correct answer is: A) Hypothyroidism

It is important that as an EMT you take note of a patient's hypothermic condition, and you should do that on the basis of the patient's temperature and also a home or apartment's temperature.

In any case, you should have recognized that this is a patient with hypothyroidism from the presence of Synthroid among her medications, a medical condition where the function of the thyroid is slow and ends up generating only minimal metabolism at the cellular level. Thus, it is understandable that the patient's temperature has dropped correspondingly.

In this case, there is no chance of atrial fibrillation, hypertension or seizures having led to the patient's hypothermic state.

35. A patient who has peptic ulcers is treated with medications like:

The correct answer is: D) Antibiotics

According to authoritative statistics, 80 percent of peptic ulcer cases are a result of H-pylori, which is the Helicobacter pylori bacteria, which damages the stomach's mucosal lining meant to protect the stomach or the duodenum. Without protection, gastric acids meant for food digestion end up damaging these areas of the body, and as a result, ulcerations develop within the tissues and mucosal lining.

You can use antibiotic treatment for controlling the H-pylori bacteria population, and also for treating the ulcerative ailment. Sometimes inflammation can be exacerbated by the use of anti-inflammatory medicines that are non-steroidal such as aspirin because they tend to increase the production of acid in the stomach.

You can rely on calcium channel blockers to treat GERD, decreasing spasms within the esophageal sphincter's lower half, but they are not recommended for use in peptic ulcer management.

36. Regarding the 17-year-old teenager with shortness of breath:

The correct answer is: C) Spontaneous pneumothorax

Patients who have Marfan's syndrome often develop spontaneous pneumothoraxes. This syndrome mainly affects a person's connective tissue, resulting in the organs and tissue structures becoming weak. Together with pneumothoracies of a spontaneous nature, such patients are also prone to aortic aneurysms.

37. Insulin has a physiological role in enhancing how well the cells utilize glucose. What happens to someone whose insulin level is low?

The correct answer is: D) Glucose remains outside the cells, and nothing can break it down.

Insulin is a hormone with the role of carrying glucose up to the cells, where it is metabolized and converted to become energy. When the level of insulin in the body is significantly low, the amount of sugar that ends up being metabolized is critically low, and consequently, the cells cannot function as well as they should.

38. The call that has come in requires that you respond to a teenager at a juvenile detention center who, you're told, has just given himself an opiate injection. Which drug below is in the opiate category?

The correct answer is: B) Heroin

Heroin is in the class of opiates, and although the other drugs can be abused, none of them is classified as an opiate.

39. At a resort on a mountaintop is a patient who complains of suddenly being short of breath and coughing. After assessing the patient, you realize there are basilar crackles in the lungs and the patient is anxious. The patient's vitals indicate heart rate is 136 and respiration is 28, while blood pressure is 176/94 mmHg. What diagnosis would you give this particular patient as assessed in the field?
The correct answer is: A) A case of high altitude pulmonary edema

High altitude pulmonary edema, abbreviated as HAPE, often develops when the affected person is unacclimated and begins a rapid ascent to altitudes exceeding 8,000 feet. The condition develops following a rise in pulmonary pressure, as well as hypertension that is a result of changes in the blood flow at high altitudes.

40. 'Status epilepticus' means a seizure:

The correct answer is: D) Is known to start just as another seizure ends before the affected patient can regain consciousness.

You can define 'status epilepticus' as a seizure lasting beyond 10 minutes, or as a kind of seizure that starts immediately just as another one stops, even without the patient first regaining consciousness. Such seizures are an emergency since there is the risk of the person sustaining fractures and airway occlusion, and sometimes, death.

41. As you transport a patient with night sweats and fever that is mild, who also has some productive cough, he mentions he has been receiving treatment from the Department of Health for a condition of a respiratory nature. Which is the most appropriate way of transporting the patient to a medical facility?

The correct answer is: B) Putting a mask on him or her as well as on the attendant EMT

There is a chance this patient has tuberculosis (TB) and so it is important that he wears a surgical mask, or alternatively, a non-breather mask. This is to protect the people providing health care and to avoid spreading of the illness.

42. Vital signs indicate the patient has gone into the shock stage described as being 'decompensated.' What are those signs?

The correct answer is: D) The heart rate is 128 and respirations are 26 while blood pressure is 82/62 mmHg

A patient reaches the physiological shock stage after precapillary sphincters guarding capillary beds on the peripheral relax after a person's blood chemistry changes. Once the sphincters open, they permit blood flow back, and it enters the capillary beds that happen to be stagnant, decreasing the volume of blood available to accomplish core perfusion. Vascular resistance of a systemic nature then drops significantly as a consequence.

43. You have a patient who believes his illness is about to kill him, and so you are not making much headway in trying to get details from him regarding his symptoms. Which technique is acceptable to use as you interview him?

The correct answer is: A) Reiterate any useful information he has provided and then ask for more.

You need to reiterate what you have understood about the patient's situation for the patient to hear because that triggers a memory of what else of relevance they may not have said. Normally it is not recommended that EMTs assume an authoritarian position when dealing with patients, as it may end up adding to the patient's distress and worsen their emotional status as well as their capacity to communicate effectively.

At the same time, it is not advisable to give false assurance to a patient like promising them they will be fully healed. Reducing physical distance between you and the patient might intimidate the patient, as will informing the patient that there is a likelihood of the illness becoming exacerbated in the absence of vital information. The latter two are techniques that can end up increasing the patient's apprehension, resulting in much poorer communication.

44. You have been sent to attend to a 65-year-old man who has brain cancer and is short of breath. What is the most appropriate action to take considering this patient has in place an order for Do Not Resuscitate (DNR)?

The correct answer is: B) Give oxygen to the patient and then transport him to a suitable emergency unit.

Even in situations where a DNR is in place, the patient needs to be made comfortable since that is his right. That is why this particular patient needs to be given oxygen as well as other pain medications.

As far as conferring with family is concerned, it is the patient's prerogative to make decisions of a medical nature relating to him unless the family actually has power of attorney, in which case they may opt to have the patient transported. It is important to note that it is the right of every patient to be dignified as he or she dies.

45. When attending to a patient whose fingers have suffered frostbite, how best can you prepare those fingers for transportation?

The correct answer is: B) Wrap the patient's fingers one by one

It is important to wrap every finger independently when you have a patient with fingers with frostbite because that ensures the fingers do not freeze together, which could cause additional damage.

It is fine to submerge the patient's digits in water that is room temperature, as long as that move does not lead to the fingers freezing again. Note that fingers with frostbite should not ever be subjected to massage as it will cause any sharp crystals of ice to penetrate the cells, killing any affected cells.

46. Which of the choices below does not cause seizures?

The correct answer is: C) Diabetes

Diabetes comes with several secondary complications, and also co-morbid medical issues that are of a chronic nature. Nevertheless, diabetes does not cause seizures. Seizures can happen after a person has sustained head injuries, but in many cases, such seizures occur during the recovery stage.

Seizures also occur following withdrawal from opioids, when a person who has been using that drug quits or has used Narcan, which is an antagonist.

47. What would be your major concern if you found someone having seizures?

The correct answer is: D) What is the patency of the airway?

Any time you have a patient actively seizing, every single muscle ends up contracting in an erratic manner, and that happens with no coordination whatsoever. For that reason, respiration is not effective at all. With every contraction of every single muscle, the demand for oxygen rises, and so the patient will remain oxygen deficient. Sometimes the patient also experiences obstruction of the airway, either partial or complete.

48. You have a patient who has had epileptic fits in the past, and this time, according to his family, he has failed to recover as he usually does. The patient suffers another seizure just as you are assessing him. What is the term given to such a condition?

The correct answer is: B) Status epilepticus

Any second or other subsequent seizures that a patient has without first waking up is put in the category of 'status epilepticus,' a serious medical condition. Hypoxia at the secondary level leads to extra cerebral irritation as well as ectopic foci propagation that ends up causing even more seizures.

49. There is a form of seizure that causes the patient to simply stare into space and not experience massive muscular contractions. What is it called?

The correct answer is: A) Petit mal

People generally think a petit mail is a failure to have any seizures. These form of seizures are common with patients of a young age, and they stare into space without having any muscular contractions. These particular seizures are usually brief, and ordinarily, you find no period of a postictal nature. The affected patient just comes to and recognizes that something has happened.

50. As an EMT, it is not uncommon to encounter cases of allergic reaction, and this is not surprising as many people with allergies are bound to find themselves exposed to the nuisance allergens at one time or another. The process of exposing someone to an allergen is termed_____.

The correct answer is: C) Sensitization

Sensitization is the process involving an antigen entering the body after which a person develops an immune response, with antibodies being produced to protect the person from the invasion.

Those antibodies assist in protecting the affected person from overreacting to the particular antigen, so the person ends up with a reaction described as 'anaphylactic.' Such a reaction can be so great when someone is exposed to an allergen for the very first time that it comes across as full-blown anaphylaxis.

51. One of the entry routes below is the most common as far as anaphylactic reaction causes are concerned. Which is it?

The correct answer is: D) Injection.

In many cases, patients are exposed to allergens through injections, specifically injections of medicine using a syringe, by an insect sting or an animal bite.

52. Once EMTs arrive at the emergency scene, their initial concern with regards to the patient is:

The correct answer is: B) Is the airway swelling and is the effort of a respiratory nature?

What you should take as your basic concern as an EMT is edema of the airway as well as bronchial edema or constriction, where edema is used in reference to an airway being reactive. Patients will die if their airway isn't working, or when they cannot ventilate. Such patients will become hypoxic, and that could lead to brain damage or death.

53. Anaphylactic shock is a kind of distributive shock, and in this case, the blood vessels are:

The correct answer is: A) Dilated

Owing to the release of chemicals from a person's immune system, there is constricting of the bronchioles, and that leads to a person's blood vessels dilating, and blood pressure therefore drops. The person's capillaries end up becoming permeable, and they leak a little bit, leading to the development of hives on a person's skin.

When working away from a hospital environment, it is not easy to recognize distributive shock, even as the patient's heart rate is low and the skin looks flushed owing to the dilating of blood vessels.

54. Following appropriate control of a patient's airway in an emergency situation, administration of epinephrine should follow next. Why is epinephrine preferable?

The correct answer is: D) All of the above.

Epinephrine has Alpha 1 and 2 effects, as well as Beta 1 and 2 effects. The stimulation from Alpha 1 leads to vaso-constriction, and the effect of this is counteraction of the distributive shock. Alpha 2 ends up regulating constriction of vessels while Beta 1 works by stimulating the patient's heart rate, and ultimately increasing cardiac output. The effect of stimulation by Beta 2 is dilating of the person's bronchioles, which aims at counteracting the airway syndrome that is of a reactive nature.

55. Syncope is caused by different things. When does a patient experience a syncopal episode?

The correct answer is: B) Upon standing

In most cases, episodes of a syncopal nature happen as the patient is standing in what can be termed 'postural hypotension.' In such instances, blood has been collecting or pooling within the appendages, and the moment that patient stands up there is a drop in cardiac output and, as a result, the person passes out.

56. There are different entry routes through which accidental poisoning can happen. Which among those possible routes is most common?

The correct answer is: C) Ingestion

Ingestion is a leading cause of accidental poisoning, and it is most prevalent among children as they eat or drink things they shouldn't. It is normal for small children to explore using the world their mouths and, unfortunately, some of the things they eat or drink end up being a hazard to them.

57. There are many poisons that adversely affect people, but there are only a handful of antidotes. What, then, can one use as a treatment when there is a case of poisoning, but an antidote is not available?

The correct answer is: B) Limitation of absorption

In the event the poison concerned has no known antidote, then all that an EMT or any other medical personnel can do is limit the quantity of poison being absorbed into the body. You can use activated charcoal to absorb poisons that a patient has ingested, and you can also reduce the rate by which poisons in powder form are absorbed. Such poisons can also be prevented from being absorbed fast by using large quantities of water to flush them. Having worked on the reduction of the absorption rate, you can then begin treating the symptoms.

58. How does poisonous ingestion happen in children?

The correct answer is: A) Mostly by accident

In most instances, children accidentally ingest poisonous substances while exploring using their mouths. The moment they come across something that is new to them, they want to taste it.

59. There are people who inhale poison to get high. What is the term used for such people?

The correct answer is: D) Huffers.

People huff by putting a quantity of a chemical, glue, paint or cleaner into a paper bag, and then place that bag over the mouth or nose and inhale deeply. This action leads to an anoxic response within the person's brain, which leads to dilation of all of their blood vessels. What the huffer experiences is an immediate euphoria, but thereafter the head begins to pound with pain.

60. Diagnosing food poisoning away from a hospital environment can be difficult because there is a wide range of symptoms associated with food poisoning. It may take quite some time after food poisoning for the affected person to fall ill. Below is a list of ailments that are all foodborne apart from one. Which is it?

The correct answer is: C) Encephalitis

Encephalitis is a brain infection that is often viral. The remaining choices are foodborne illnesses.

61. What is the common pulse for a newborn child?

The correct answer is: (A) 140 to 160

140 to 160 beats per minute is the common pulse rate for newborns.

62. For a child ages 1 to 6, what is the common pulse rate?

The correct answer is: C) 100 to 120 bpm

Children ages 1 to 6 have a pulse rate of 100 to 120 bpm.

63. What is the common pulse rate for a kid over 6 years old?

The correct answer is: (D) 80 to 100

Older children, over age six, are more in the region of 80 to 100.

64. What is the accurate blood flow from the heart through the lungs?

The correct answer is: (A) Superior/inferior venae cava through the right atrium to the right ventricle, through the lungs to the left atrium and left ventricle, then finally to the aorta

The blood goes in the heart through the inferior/superior venae cava and then to the right atrium, down to the right ventricle. Passing through the pulmonary vein, the blood goes to the lungs, coming back through the left atrium and left ventricle, then through the aorta.

65. The angina pectoris has a distinct dissimilarity with a myocardial infarction. What is it?

The correct answer is: (D) Constant mental and physical stress causes angina pectoris

The root of angina pectoris is generally stress, whether mental or physical, with signs for a short period of time–maximum 10 minutes. Usually, rest is the cure.

66. You find an 80-year-old male patient experiencing shortness of breath. What is the most unlikely cause of his distress?

The correct answer is: (D) URTI

If the patient was experiencing all the health conditions described except for D) URTI, he could experience these types of symptoms. URTI means Upper Respiratory Tract

Infection, and it would be the least likely to cause the man shortness of breath without other accompanying ailments.

67. On the right side of the heart, there is a three-flapped valve. What is the valve?

The correct answer is: (C) The tricuspid valve

The tricuspid valve is also the partition between the right ventricle and the right atrium.

68. The sole purpose of the mitral valve is?

The correct answer is: (B) Stopping the flow of blood back to the left atrium

The location of the mitral valve is between the ventricle and left atrium, hence blocking blood flow back to the atrium.

69. A clinician finds that his patient is experiencing some discomfort in his chest and puts him in a comfortable position. What should the clinician do next to assist the 45-year-old male?

The correct answer is: (C) Using an NRB mask, administer the oxygen at 15 liters every minute

Every patient that experiences chest discomfort must always be administered oxygen. In this case, ventilation is not required since no information has been given to show that it is needed.

70. What should you do first when a 62-year-old patient with a history of heart illness complains that he is suffering from chest pains?

The correct answer is: (D)Administer a lot of oxygen after putting the patient in a comfortable position

The very first step should be administering oxygen and placing the patient in a comfortable posture. Then ask the patient if you can help him take nitroglycerin if it's not contraindicated. To make sure he isn't in cardiogenic shock, assess his vital signs. The AED pads should not be put on a patient that is awake and has a heartbeat. The

AED pads do not monitor the heart rhythm like the ALS providers' electrodes; they have a different purpose.

71. Ventricular fibrillation is often from the conversion of which heart rhythm?

The correct answer is: (B) Ventricular tachycardia

Ventricular tachycardia more often than not transforms into ventricular fibrillation which is a very dangerous rhythm that is corrected by the AED.

72. The pain in a cardiac arrest is usually defined as which of these characteristics by the patients?

The correct answer is: (B) The feel of being squeezed and/or crushed

As many heart attack victims describe it, the pain is a crushing and squeezing force which is released towards the upper back and arms. However, myocardial pain is often hard to distinguish as it occurs in many different forms.

73. The following are patients with various signs and symptoms; which indicates cardiac compromise?

The correct answer is: (C) A 53-year-old female experiencing sudden perspiration, dull chest pain and breathing complications

These are typical indications of a cardiac compromise.

74. Among the four chambers of the heart, which one pumps blood rich in oxygen to the rest of the body?

The correct answer is: (D) Left ventricle

From the lungs, blood rich in oxygen gets to the left atrium through the pulmonary veins and then is pumped to the body via the left ventricle.

75. If you are alone and find yourself in a situation where a 64-year-old woman has collapsed due to a heart attack, what is the next action to take after assessment and administration of two ventilations?

The correct answer is: (A) Analyze the heart rhythm and, if specified, give a shock

Overwhelming data shows that defibrillating early provides the best chance for correcting the most common reason for heart attacks—ventricular fibrillation. This overshadows the limited information that people in prolonged durations of heart attack may benefit from cardiopulmonary resuscitation before defibrillation.

76. Upon arrival at a scene, you discover a patient whose mental status has been altered. After a quick scan, which of these items would help in pointing to the likely cause for his agitated state of mind?

The correct answer is: (B) Medication for depression, anxiety and hypertension

A survey of the scene will lead to important hints about what might be the matter with the patient. Various medications for particular illnesses will provide even more accurate insight. These not only provide the clinician with the patient's medical past but also show where to begin assessing and investigating the patient's symptoms.

77. When the patient isn't responsive to your loud verbal stimuli and you come across these medications—Lipitor and Glucophage—what is the most likely source of the problem?

The correct answer is: (C) Reaction caused by diabetes

The Glucophage points you in the right direction since it is a diabetes medication. Even so, identification of the kind of reaction the patient is experiencing will require further evaluation. Lipitor might be needed in the long-term, but elevated cholesterol normally has zero effect on mental status in the way hyper or hypoglycemia do.

78. What would be your primary field diagnosis if your neurological evaluation of a patient that is not responding reveals pinpoint pupils?

The correct answer is: (D) Narcotics

Narcotics are the only drugs mentioned here that would cause constriction of the pupils; thus, pinpoint. The rest of the drugs listed have no effect on the pupils but may cause a disoriented state of mind.

79. With a diabetic patient that gets almost 4 injections of insulin a day and has 18 breaths each minute, what would be the most likely reason he was found unresponsive, tachycardic and diaphoretic?

The correct answer is: (A) Hypoglycemia

A diabetic patient dependent on insulin with the stated symptoms is highly likely to be hypoglycemic. The diaphoresis and tachycardia are from a catecholamine release trying to mobilize more glucose. It is likely that the patient has high blood pressure, but that isn't the cause for unresponsiveness.

80. A clinician would give 15 grams oral instant glucose to a diabetic patient that is experiencing hypoglycemia, but not if the patient is _____

The correct answer is: (C) Half-awake without being able to swallow

A patient that cannot swallow should never be given anything by mouth as aspiration is a huge risk. Glucose should be given to a patient with an altered mental state and blood sugar of 80mg/dl so as to rectify their state of mind.

81. Which one of these is the first sign of diabetes in a lot of young patients and is often a fatal complication?

The correct answer is: (D) Diabetic ketoacidosis (DKA)

More often than not, the first symptom of diabetes is Diabetic Ketoacidosis. When there isn't fuel—glucose—for the cells to burn, they will burn fat, and fat doesn't necessarily burn clean. The burning will produce acids that build up and, if not treated vigorously, this condition can be fatal. High blood pressure and heart diseases are deep-rooted diabetes problems.

82. Apart from thirst, acetone on the breath, frequent urination, poor skin turgor, dry skin, altered mental status and confusion, which other indications are involved with diabetic ketoacidosis (DKA)?

The correct answer is: (B) The appearance of intoxication

Because of the hyperglycemia, the glucose undergoes dieresis by the kidneys, so it's removed from the bloodstream, making the patient more dehydrated. While the blood thickens, the heart output decreases, causing the organ to work a lot harder. With the excess glucose and unfinished combustion from the other various sources of fuel, the patient appears intoxicated due to brain impairment.

83. The more common of the two kinds of CVA is the ischemic stroke. Which of these is the other kind?

The correct answer is: (B) Hemorrhagic stroke

A hemorrhagic stroke, also known as a bleed, is the other type of cerebral vascular accident, while embolic and thrombotic strokes are types of ischemic strokes that involve normal blood flow being halted by a clot. Lastly, a TIA is more often than not just called a mini stroke, which is a precursor to a complete cerebral vascular accident.

84. When the diagnosis of a condition is a TIA, the symptoms must resolve within 24 hours _____?

The correct answer is: (D) Without any permanent reactions

TIAs are often precursors to a major stroke, which is why they're referred to as mini strokes. Most are resolved in 15 minutes. For a stroke to be diagnosed as a TIA, all symptoms and signs have to resolve within 24 hours.

85. Between the Cincinnati Stroke Scale and the Los Angeles Pre-hospital Stroke Screen, which tool uses arm drift as a diagnostic tool in the assessment of a patient with stroke?
The correct answer is: (B) Cincinnati Stroke Scale

The arm-drift maneuver is used in the Cincinnati Stroke Scale as a tool for diagnosis. The clinician asks the patient to lift their arms in front of them and close their eyes. Then he watches for an arm to drift downward. If a downward drift occurs, the clinician is to assess for a CVA on that side.

86. Symptoms of a stroke are often similar to other various medical problems, and so, in order to prevent administering the wrong treatment, it is mandatory to work through the differences. An example is how hypoglycemia is usually confused for a cerebral vascular accident. How would one rule out the difference?

The correct answer is: (B) Checking blood sugar

The use of a glucometer for a blood sugar checkup is one of the simplest and most often overlooked diagnostic tool. The rest of the screening information in this question does not confirm or discard hypoglycemia as a diagnosis.

87. Rapid transport to the stroke center is by far a clinician's preferred method of treatment and assessment for a stroke patient. Which of these presents the perfect timing for this from the beginning of the indications till treatment?

The correct answer is: (B) Three hours

The outcome is better with a quicker return of the blood flow when there has been a restriction of it. There is a significant possibility that all deficits will resolve without lasting effects if tPA is applied within three hours of the emergence of the symptoms.

88. Which of these statements about indications of a stroke would make a clinician highly suspicious?

The correct answer is: (A) This is the worst headache I have ever had.

The statement should not be disregarded or considered to be dramatic; it should instead make the clinician adjust their evaluation, so it is inclusive of a hemorrhagic stroke. All other statements in the answer choices make clear the potency of the headache and might not necessarily eliminate the possibility of a stroke. However, disclosure of the worst headache one's ever had should definitely be an alert to something bigger than simply a headache.

89. Which of these is the medical condition whereby a patient experiences seizure activity or convulsions from time to time?

The correct answer is: (D) Epilepsy.

In this medical condition, the patient suffers from seizures often. The postictal state is usually the duration after a convulsion in which a patient is possibly unresponsive because the brain is resting and resetting and therefore slow to respond or possibly unresponsive. Tonic-clonic and focal motor are just types of seizure activity.

90. During assessment, which of these highly suggests that a depressed patient is at risk of suicide?

The correct answer is: (A) An unsuccessful suicide attempt from before

This is particularly indicative of a suicide risk if a patient has a history of suicide attempts. Also, people considering suicide often give away belongings. Hostility directed to family in itself isn't necessarily a sign for suicide. High blood pressure is usually treatable with medications and change in lifestyle.

91. When blood is pumped out of the heart through the heart's right ventricle, where does it go?

The correct answer is: (D) Pulmonary arteries first, and then the lungs.

Deoxygenated blood reaches the right atrium and is then pumped out from the right ventricle through the pulmonary arteries to the lungs.

92. According to research, the biggest cause of shocks inappropriately delivered by Automated External Defibrillators (AEDs) is as a result of _____.

Correct answer is: (D) Human error

The majority of shocks inappropriately administered have been linked to human errors, like the use of the AED when a vehicle is in motion, or the device is used on a patient who has a pulse.

93. Which of the statements below is correct when it comes to assessing cardiac-compromised patients?

The correct answer is: (A) The extent of any cardiac damage cannot be determined in the field.

It is not possible to know the severity of damaged tissue in the field. Therefore the reason for focused assessment is to collect information for the facility that will receive the patient. Always ask about medications. A focused history is not linked to the use of an AED. Cardiac pains have many presentations which make it very difficult to distinguish them from other conditions.

94. Which of the statements below is true regarding the heart's left atrium?

The correct answer is: (B) The pulmonary vein delivers blood to the left atrium.

Blood that is oxygenated in the lungs returns to the heart's left atrium through the pulmonary veins, where it moves to the heart's left ventricle which then pumps it to the other parts of the body.

95. AED pads are best applied to patients when they

The correct answer is: (C) Are apneic and don't have a pulse

AEDs should not be applied unless a patient has no pulse and no respirations.

96. What do you call the two chambers on the lower side of the heart?

The correct answer is: (A) Ventricles

Both the lower right and left chambers of the heart are known as "ventricles."

97. Which valve is located between the heart's right atrium and ventricle?

The correct answer is: (B) Tricuspid valve

The tricuspid valve is located in between the heart's right atrium and ventricle.

98. You arrive at the scene with an elderly male patient complaining of extreme chest pains. He has a history of heart problems. In such a scenario, what is the role medical direction plays?

The correct answer is: (B) To authorize interventions

The primary role of medical direction is to authorize the EMT to deliver interventions to the patient.

99. You arrive at the scene with an elderly male patient complaining of extreme chest pains. He has a history of heart problems. Without more medical direction, what dosage of nitroglycerin should be given at most?

The correct answer is: (B) 3 tablets

Without more medical direction, the maximum dose that can be administered is three tablets or three sprays.

100.　　You arrive at the scene with an elderly male patient complaining of extreme chest pains and experiencing difficulty breathing. He is overweight and is a high-capacity chain smoker. Which condition is he likely to have?

The correct answer is: (A) Coronary artery disease

There are a number of conditions that the patient could have. However, it is most likely that he has coronary artery disease.

101.　　You arrive at the scene with a young male patient who has a rapid pulse. When questioned, the patient says that he was only running. With this information, what are your first thoughts?

The correct answer is: (B) The patient's reaction is normal.

The patient's rapid pulse is to be expected given the fact that he was running.

102.   You arrive at the scene with an elderly female patient whose heart has stopped. After administering one AED shock, she starts breathing but at only 15 breaths a minute and the carotid pulse is very strong. What do you do next?

The correct answer is: (B) Provide additional oxygen via NRB

Once the patient starts breathing and regains her pulse, the next action should be providing additional oxygen via NRB. A bag-valve-mask should be used to assist if the respiratory rate falls below or above the maximum and minimum limits.

103.   You arrive at the scene to find a male patient who is 50 years of age having cardiac problems. What will happen if his heartbeat is too fast or slow?

The correct answer is:(B) He might lose consciousness.

If the patient is too tachycardic or bradycardic, he may lose consciousness due to insufficient perfusion.

104.   You arrive at the scene to find a female patient who is 53 years of age and experiencing severe chest pains. You have administered one tablet after getting medical direction to administer nitroglycerin. What should you do next?

The correct answer is: (B) Check the patient's blood pressure

After a dose of nitroglycerin is administered and before another dose is administered, the patient's blood pressure should be checked since nitroglycerin acts as a vasodilator.

105.   You are sent to a male patient who is 50 years of age and is experiencing severe chest pains. To give nitroglycerin, which of the following is a contraindication?

The correct answer is:(D) The patient's systolic BP is below 100

Nitroglycerin should only be administered if the patient has a systolic BP less than 100 since it is a vasodilator and may cause blood pressure to drop to dangerous levels.

106.   You are at the scene where a patient has just fallen from atop a ladder. When caring for the patient, what should not be taken into consideration?

The correct answer is: A) The length of the ladder

The length of the ladder is not important when making your assessment since the patient may have been at any point of the ladder before he fell and not necessarily at the top.

107.   You arrive at a motor vehicle accident where there are three patients with visible but minor injuries. Two of the patients refuse treatment, while the third one complains of back and neck pains. What should be your next course of action?

The correct answer is: D) Treat the patient with neck and back pains as your partner gets the other two patients to sign refusals.

Patient refusals must not only be informed but also be in writing. Any forcible treatment of patients is considered battery.

108.   You have a male patient who is 17 years of age who was found facedown in the swimming pool. Currently, he is still in the pool, being held with his face above the water. He is breathing, with a steady pulse, although he is still unconscious. How should you proceed?

The correct answer is: C) Get in the pool and apply spinal and cervical immobilization.

Spinal precautions are necessary since you have no knowledge of what caused the patient to lose consciousness.

109.   When a laceration spurts bright red blood, which kind of injury does it usually point to?

The correct answer is: B) Artery injuries

The brightness of the blood indicates it is highly oxygenated. The most oxygenated blood is found in the arteries as it comes directly from the heart.

110.   You have a patient with a laceration on his right leg that has reached the femoral artery. Blood is still soaking past the bandages even though you've made sure there is pressure applied directly to the wound. What is the best course of action?

The correct answer is: B) Elevate the leg.

Lifting the leg to a point where it is higher than the heart may help to reduce the bleeding. If that doesn't help, the next course of action is to use the pressure point above the wound. New bandages should be applied over the old ones.

111.   In a motor vehicle crash with impact to the front, the driver wasn't restrained, the steering wheel is bent and the windshield is spidered. What type of energy transfer was there?

The correct answer is: D) Blunt

Blunt-force trauma is not limited to gunshots or stab wounds. It includes any injuries caused whenever energy is transferred to the body by having something penetrate it. Deceleration injuries like a car's front-end collision with a tree can cause blunt-force trauma.

112.   How would you classify a penetrating missile that is traveling at speeds exceeding 2,000 feet per second?

The correct answer is: C) High velocity

A projectile traveling faster than 2,000 feet per second is deemed high velocity as it has a high probability to cause a transfer of kinetic energy. Examples would be rifle rounds that can send large projectiles over long distances and have devastating effects.

113.   A permanent cavity is formed when a projectile contacts the tissues during penetrating trauma. How do temporary cavities develop?

The correct answer is: B) By energy scrubbed off from the projectile.

As a projectile travels through space, it gives energy off as air molecules are pushed away. Kinetic energy transfers to the human tissue from the projectile upon impact. If the projectile is high velocity, the tissue that absorbs the energy is damaged in most cases, but the disruption is usually not enough to cause permanent damage.

114. _____ often refers to the way the patient was injured.

The correct answer is: A) Mechanism of injuries

Mechanism of injury will transfer energy to a patient, resulting in a predictable injury pattern. The manner in which one gets injured is known as the mechanism of injury. The clinician is now able to predict the patient's injuries (type) and how they may respond to treatment. Mechanisms of injury also help in predicting injury patterns.

115. What is the first thing you should do when you approach a trauma incident scene?

The correct answer is: D) Ensure the scene is safe

Ensuring the scene is safe is the first thing you should do when you approach an incident scene. You will not be able to help those you have been called to assist if you get injured yourself. Moreover, you will complicate matters by becoming an additional victim. Isolating bodily fluids is important once you have safely arrived at the scene and approached the patient. The next steps after you find your patient are airway and C-spine control.

116. When a lot of blood collects under the skin, this is referred to as _____.

The correct answer is: C) A hematoma

When large blood vessels are damaged, a lot of blood collects under the skin, and it is referred to as a hematoma. This is usually found between tissue layers. A smaller collection of blood within a tissue such as the dermis is known as a contusion. A bruise is used generically to refer to both contusions and hematomas.

117. You have a trauma patient whose left hand is caught in a conveyor belt in between rollers. It takes you 30 minutes to extricate the hand. During extrication, you observed that there was a delay in capillary refill distal to the injury. After extrication, you observe rapid capillary refill distal mid-palm to the deformity of the injury. There are no lacerations, no visible fractures and slight swelling. You know there are many

problems that may occur as a result of crush injuries. Which of the choices below is not a complication of crush injuries?

The correct answer is: C) No injury at all

Crush injuries occur when pressure is applied to tissue by two objects. If the pressure is applied over a long time, it causes tissue damage resulting in fractures, anaerobic injuries and lacerations. Reversion to anaerobic metabolism generating lactic and pyruvic acids may result when there is no blood flow and the tissue does not receive oxygen. As time continues, more tissue is damaged, releasing more acids and other byproducts caused by incomplete metabolism. Unattended, this causes more swelling, problems with coagulation, tissue loss and death.

118.   What would you call and injury when a patient loses the distal third of their lower extremity?

The correct answer is: D) Amputation

The loss of part or a full extremity is referred to as amputation. Tissue loss from any part is referred to as avulsion. Any tissue that is lost should be protected with a wet/moist dressing and put in cold saline.

119.   It is important to control bleeding whenever there is damaged tissue that causes bleeding due to a traumatic event. Which steps should you follow to control the bleeding?

The correct answer is: B) Direct pressure, digital pressure, elevation, and tourniquet

Applying direct pressure should be done first as it stops 90 percent of bleeding injuries. If this fails, then the next action should be to apply digital pressure. Elevation should be done next and finally, in cases of excessive or uncontrolled bleeding, a tourniquet should be applied. Pressure dressings can only be applied when the bleeding is under control and fully stopped.

120.   You have a trauma patient who is 16 years of age and has what seems to be a femur fracture located mid-shaft. You see a laceration directly above where the fracture is suspected to be and the bleeding is under control. Which type of fracture could this be?

The correct answer is: D) Open

Whenever there is open skin above a fracture, these are referred to as open fractures. Greensticks are usually found where bones are not completely ossified, mainly in children. Comminuted fractures are caused by extreme forces that cause many more smaller fractures within the original fracture site.

121.   On the way to a hospital, a patient is intubated. When assessing the placement of the tube, you hear wheezing within the lungs. What is the most likely cause of the sound?

The correct answer is: D) An inhalation injury affecting the lower air-conducting passages

An inhalation injury that occurs in the lower airway can cause wheezing and bronchospasm while an inhalation injury that occurs in the upper airways can cause a hoarse voice and a high-pitched wheezing sound caused by disrupted airflow. When one inhales byproducts of combustion, there is also a probability of a wheezing sound, and it is still considered an injury of the lower air-conducting passages.

122.   Which step among the following should a paramedic perform last after immobilizing an extreme fracture of the lower right arm?

The correct answer is: C) Assess the distal motor presence and sensory plus perfusion

When one immobilizes any fracture, they are assessing the status of the distal motor, perfusion and sensory. This is done to make sure that there was no additional injury that occurred during the immobilization process. An injury can occur when the splint is put on incorrectly. If paramedics realize that an additional injury occurred during the process, they ought to reexamine the splinting process and correct any faults that may have occurred.

123.   On this question where a 24-year-old female has a gunshot wound at the back:

The correct answer is: C) Cardiac tamponade

Cardiac tamponade causes a decrease in the cardiac output and this is evidenced by pale skin and hypotension. Other signs of cardiac tamponade include difficulties in respiration, tachycardia and bluish discoloration of the arms, neck and face. When one has a pneumothorax owing to a wound within their chest or blood pools in the pleural cavity, there will be a decrease in breathing sounds.

124.   When treating a 12-year-old male patient who has had a hit from some baseball, the correct treatment sequence is:

The correct answer is: D) Ensure the patient sits upright and leans forward while putting pressure on the nose

Putting pressure on the nares is the correct technique to control nose bleeding. It is crucial, too, to ensure the patient leans forward to reduce the chances of blood going down the throat. However, a patient should not be made to lean forward if they have a history of spinal injuries.

125.   The most appropriate treatment to give an elderly patient who fell an injured her knee is:

The correct answer is: A) Secure the patient on a backboard before cushioning her appropriately

A patient who has a fracture of the femur should be immobilized on the backboard and cushioned appropriately. Inflation of the patient's legs with PASG is not necessary. The use of traction splinting is only appropriate if the fracture occurs at the mid-shaft, while the use of cushioned boarded splints will not offer adequate immobilization.

126.   Which of the following types of patients is most suitable to be referred for triage to a center that does not deal with trauma?

The correct answer is: C) A 25-year-old woman who has a one-inch cut on the thigh

Among the four patients, she is the only one who has an isolated injury and therefore can be treated in a non-trauma center. The others require detailed assessment and hence are fit for a trauma center.

127.   On the question of the 37-year-old male who cut his leg in his backyard, medical treatments you should prioritize include ...

The correct answer is: A) Continuing to apply pressure directly on the patient's wound as you seek ALS support.

For this patient, applying pressure directly to the wound and offering him fluids gives him the best chances of survival.

128. In a crush injury, the most common early finding is:

The correct answer is: A) Some pain

Pain is the most common sign in a crush injury and normally it is detected early, before the other signs and symptoms.

129. The most appropriate categorization of the burns in a 26-year-old female who escaped from a house on fire is:

The correct answer is: A) Third-degree burns

The patient is most likely facing third-degree burns which affect soft tissue. These burns are normally painless except at the penumbra, where nerve stimulation is stimulation.

130. Regarding a 43-year-old man engaged in an altercation:

The correct answer is: B) Intubate the patient orally and assist his ventilations using a bag-valve-mask

This patient's face and airway are unstable. The patient's airway will require protecting as soon as possible, and that should be done using an endotracheal tube. Owing to the instability of the face, it is crucial that you place an adjunct so that the patient's airway does not get occluded due to the jaw pressure emanating from the bag-valve-mask being applied.

131. A gray or bluish skin coloration due to oxygen deficiency is referred to as

The correct answer is: (B) Cyanosis

Cyanosis is a condition that occurs when O2 saturation in the blood flowing through the arteries falls under 0.85 to 0.90. Its presence is usually seen in nail beds and lips.

132. What are you required to do for a patient whose oxygen saturation drops significantly after a few breaths of mouth-to-mouth resuscitation by use of an Ambu-bag that has been connected to 100 percent oxygen?

The correct answer is: (B)Change the patient's head position.

This is an indication that a patient does not have effective respiration. The patient's head should be positioned using the jaw thrust maneuver or chin lift/head tilt and then attempt to respirate again.

133.   What is the right amount of air required for injection into the cuff of an endotracheal tube?

The correct answer is: (C) 10 ccs

There are 10 ccs of air in a normal endotracheal tube.

134.   What is the space between the epiglottis and tongue base referred to as?

The correct answer is: (D) Vallecula.

Vallecula is important during intubation.

135.   A strange vocalization, difficult breathing and gasping are all characteristics of which condition?

The correct answer is: (A) Agonal breaths

Agonal breaths are common in patients with cardiac arrest and at times may persist for some minutes after the end of a heartbeat.

136.   What is the longest time an intubation attempt can take?

The correct answer is: (B) 30 seconds

In case of an unsuccessful intubation, do not attempt another intubation for at least half a minute, and then allow the patient to hyperventilate before trying again.

137.   A sound that is high pitched as a result of a turbulent flow of air in the upper airway is characteristic of which condition? It can be expiratory, inspiratory or there during expiration and inspiration.

The correct answer is: (C) Stridor

Stridor is an indication of a severe case of obstruction of the upper airway.

138.   The condition where one is unable to move sufficient air that is needed for enough perfusion is known as?

The correct answer is: (B) Respiratory failure

This is a term in medicine that refers to insufficient exchange of gases by the respiratory system. It can be indicated by observation of drops in oxygen saturation and the quality/rate of breathing.

139.   Which one of the following is the wrong technique for confirmation of the correct placement of the endotracheal tube?

The correct answer is: (B)Visualization of the chest rise and fall.

Seeing the chest move does not guarantee that there has been correct placement of the tube because stomach inflation can be mistaken for rising of the chest.

140.   The tubes that carry air to and from the lungs are referred to as?

The correct answer is: (A) Bronchi

The trachea is connected to the bronchi which are then connected to the bronchioles.

141.   Stomach expansion due to excess ventilation pressure that causes the extra air to enter the stomach as opposed to the lungs is referred to as what?

The correct answer is: (B) Gastric distention

One should avoid gastric distention as it causes vomiting.

142.   Which sign is not an indication of breathing adequately?

The correct answer is: (C)Breathing that has been limited to the muscles of the abdomen.

Using the muscles of the abdomen in breathing is an indication of difficulty breathing and not an indication of sufficient breathing.

143.   Observing a patient's _____ can help in detecting whether the patient is suffering from cyanosis.

The correct answer is: (C) Nail beds

Cyanosis' early indications are usually present on the lips and in the beds of nails.

144.   A nasal and oral airway should:

The correct answer is: (C) Be useful in preventing the tongue from causing an airway blockage.

When unconscious, a patient's tongue tends to slip to the back of the mouth causing an airway blockage which can be prevented by using a nasal or oral airway.

145.   Name the medication that increases breathing effectiveness and opens bronchioles in patients suffering from shortness of breath.

The correct answer is: (A) Bronchodilators

A bronchodilator is used in dilation or widening of the bronchioles and thereby allows airflow with more ease. Albuterol is a common bronchodilator.

146.   You have a male patient who is 52 years old. He is suffering from dull chest pain. After assessment, you realize that the skin is clammy, cool and pale despite the fact that he is oriented and alert. What do you do next?

The correct answer is: (C)Supplementation of oxygen.

Damage of the heart muscles can be reduced by immediate administration of oxygen to a patient with cardiac problem.

147. Cardiac compromise refers to?

The correct answer is: (D)Any problem associated with the heart.

Cardiac compromise is a term that describes different types of heart problems. It helps an EMT like you in identifying a cardiac problem without having to go above the scope of your practice.

148. What do AEDs treat in patients?

The correct answer is: (A) Ventricular fibrillation

An AED is used to treat pulseless, apneic patients in ventricular fibrillation or ventricular tachycardia. AEDs are used in the treatment of pulseless, apneic patients in ventricular tachycardia or ventricular fibrillation.

149. The heart rate of a 0- to 3-month-old baby is said to be normal at?

The correct answer is: (A) 140 to 160

A newborn's normal heart rate is 140 to 160, while an infant's normal rate is 120 to 140 bpm. The heart rate of children aged between 1 to 6 years is 100 to 120 whereas children above 6 years have a heart rate of 80 to 100 bpm.

150. What is the name of the valve that has two flaps and is on the left of the heart?

The correct answer is: (C) Bicuspid valve

The valve with two flaps is known as the mitral valve, also referred to as the bicuspid valve. The valve with three flaps is known as the tricuspid valve.

151. There are three main components that make up the vascular system. Which one is not one of these components?

The correct answer is: (C) Myoglobin

The blood, heart and blood vessels are major components of the vascular system. Myoglobin forms part of the muscle. When a large muscle mass is injured, it gives off myoglobin to the bloodstream. Molecules of myoglobin are big and cause renal problems during burns, trauma or elocution.

152.   Starting from outside, which layers cover the heart?

The correct answer is: (C) Epicardium, myocardium, endocardium

The heart is surrounded by a protective sac known as the pericardium. There is a layer that is slippery that covers the heart and it is referred to as the epicardium. It helps the heart avoid friction. Pumping of blood is made possible by the myocardium when it lets electricity pass through, thereby causing the muscles to squeeze and blood to pump. The endocardium and epicardium have similar tissue. Clotting is prevented by the endocardium due to its being smooth.

153.   From the complaints below, which describes the pain of the chest that is caused by cardiac complications?

The correct answer is: (B) Bricks that weigh a ton on the chest.

Cardiovascular=related chest pains are usually referred to as pressure. Cardiac events can be ruled out on the kind of chest pains described alone. A patient could have chest pains that can be described as pains that are sharp to pulling of the muscles to toothaches. Pains that are stabbing and sharp and can be located by a finger are an indication of pulmonary embolism.

154.   Name the artery that carries blood that does not have oxygen and the vein that carries blood that has oxygen.

The correct answer is: (C) Pulmonary, pulmonary

The only artery that carries deoxygenated blood is the pulmonary artery, while the pulmonary vein is the only one that carries oxygenated blood back to the heart. Arteries carry blood rich in oxygen from the heart and the veins carry blood that is deoxygenated back to the heart. The aorta is the major artery that exits the left ventricle to the body whereas the vena cava is the one that returns blood to the right side of the heart.

155.   Which of these aren't components of blood that cause clotting?

The correct answer is: (B) Plaque

The fat deposits on the walls of arteries are called plaque. Plaque causes narrowing and hardening of the arteries. Even though clots usually form around plaques, they are not part of the process of clotting. The disks that are flat and stick together, creating the thrombus, are called platelets. The tiny strands made of fiber that make the framework of clots by strengthening them are referred to as fibrin. Formation of clotting is signaled by thrombin.

156.   You have been dispatched to the residence of a female patient. She is 46 years old and is suffering from diarrhea, nausea, abdominal cramping and vomiting. She says that she fell ill a short time after eating cheesecake. She is intolerant to lactose. Her BP test shows 136/88. Pulse is 94 bpm while the rate of respiration is 18 breaths in a minute. Before your arrival, she vomited twice. Give your diagnosis.

The correct answer is: (D) Acute gastroenteritis.

The cause of acute gastroenteritis could be ingestion of toxins, viruses, bacteria or lactose by a patient who is lactose intolerant. Symptoms and signs include diarrhea, vomiting, abdominal cramps and nausea.

157.   You have a male patient who is 32 years old and complains of a severe crushing feeling at the center of the chest and difficulty in breathing which started when he was mowing the lawn three quarters of an hour before your arrival. The pain stimuli seems to be working on him. At the moment, he has adequate ventilation, pulse is 95 percent, and his skin is cool, diaphoretic and pale. Your first action should be to give:

The correct answer is: (A) 12 to 15 liters of oxygen.

High flow of oxygen can be indicated by severe breath shortness in the first assessment as long as there is adequate ventilation. When the patient has inadequate breathing, there should be immediate institution of positive pressure ventilation with oxygen.

158.   Your patient, who is 76 years old, has swelling in the legs and is in a wheelchair. After assessment, it is confirmed that she has edema. You do a bilateral pulse palpitation. The skin is pink, dry and warm. The lungs are clear. Which of the following conditions could she be suffering from?

The correct answer is: (D) Chronic CHF.

Edema of the sacrum or legs is usually caused by right-sided congestive failure of the heart as well as ascites and jugular vein distention. Right-sided heart failure is usually caused by left-sided heart failure and the symptoms and signs are fatigue, paroxysmal nocturnal dyspnea, orthopnea and breath shortness, coughing of frothy pink sputum and a hacking, dry cough.

159.   You have a patient who is 49 years old and complaining of pain between the shoulder blades and radiating to the lower back. The pain is constant and started 10 minutes before you arrived, while the patient was eating. Told to rate the pain, the patient gives it a 10/10 and describes it as sharp and tearing. The BP is 130/76 and 78/48 in the right and left arms respectively. Pulse is 98 bpm and is regular while the rate of respiration is 20 per min and is non-labored. Which of the following conditions would you suspect?

The correct answer is: (C) Aortic dissection

Aortic dissection can be indicated by different blood pressures in both arms and a pain that is sharp and tearing between the shoulder blades. This is an emergency that calls for immediate transportation to the hospital emergency room.

160.   Death in America is mostly caused by?

The correct answer is: (A) Coronary heart disease.

Coronary heart disease is the main cause of death in America, killing approximately 466,000 people per year. Most of the factors that cause coronary heart disease are habits that people can do away with (for instance, smoking, leading a life that is sedentary or obesity). Traumatic injuries, cancer and chronic obstructive pulmonary diseases are major health issues, but not as many people die of them as compared to coronary heart disease.

161.   The highest running speed of a nasal cannula should be?

The correct answer is: D) 6 lpm.

A nasal cannula administers O2, and the rate of flow ranges from two to six LPM. This means the concentration of the O2 delivered is 28 percent to 44 percent.

162.   Identify the apparatus as described. It's intended to ease a patient's sightless intubation and comprises a cuffed double-lumen tube whose one end is blind. The cuff's rise permits this device to carry out a role as the endotracheal tube and ends the esophagus, permitting air passage as well as avoiding gastric reflux substances.

The correct answer is: B) Dual lumen airway

Combi-tube is also another name for this device.

163.   To provide oxygen therapy at "100 percent," what should be the flow rate's reading?

The correct answer is: A) 12 to 15 lpm

When 12 to 15 lpm is administered through a non-breather mask, abbreviated as NBR, it is considered to be 100 percent oxygen.

164.   A man falls from a ladder, which leads to him suffering respiratory pain. Which air passage tactic could you use?

The correct answer is: D) Jaw thrust.

The best airway opening maneuver for an ailing person that has gone through traumatic hurt is the jaw thrust.

165.   What is the name of a device which transports a certain medicine quantity towards the lungs as a small burst of aerosolized medication which is gasped down by patients?

The correct answer is: C) Metered-dose inhaler

This device is mostly used when treating asthma, COPD and other respiratory complications.

166. The air passage comprises high as well as low airways. The higher airway begins from the mouth and nares, which is concluded at _____?

The correct answer is: C) Cricoid cartilage

The air passage is split into two varying anatomical areas: the upper air passage and the lower air passage. That upper air passage begins at the point where air enters the person's body through the nose, or 'nares,' and mouth. Air has to pass via a person's nose, get filtered, and then warmed before passing through the remaining part of the upper air passage to enter the lower air passage. The airway on the upper side ends at the cricoid cartilage, which constitutes the larynx' distal end. The body's thyroid cartilage is found near the central end of a person's larynx.

167. The most common obstruction of the airway is the tongue, which drops to the back and occludes the _____?

The correct answer is: D) Pharynx.

A person's pharynx/throat can be occluded when the tongue falls back, obstructing the flow of air. As air enters a person's nostrils, the passage it follows is the nasopharynx, and thereafter it passes through the oropharynx before it goes through the person's pharynx to enter the person's trachea.

The jaw thrust or chin lift can raise the tongue so that it no longer blocks the pharynx' rear and the air passage can reopen to allow the flow of air into the person's lungs. A person's trachea is so distal that the tongue cannot occlude it.

168. A person's airway on the lower side has its end where the alveoli are found, and that is the place where exchange of gases occurs. Oxygen enters the hemoglobin through the semi-permeable membrane. The place where this occurs is _____.

The correct answer is: A) Capillary bed

In every air sac, there is a high concentration of oxygen. Therefore, there is always oxygen passing or diffusing through the membrane of the alveolar to enter the heart's pulmonary capillary. Where the pulmonary capillary starts, the red blood cells' hemoglobin contains carbon dioxide that is bound to it, but minimal oxygen. The available oxygen ends up binding itself to the hemoglobin, thereby getting rid of the carbon dioxide. Carbon dioxide is released, and parts of sodium bicarbonate are dissolved into the blood flowing through the pulmonary capillary.

The level of carbon dioxide concentration is high within the heart's pulmonary capillary. Carbon dioxide leaves the person's blood, then passes through the alveolar membrane and enters the air sacs. It is the kind of exchange that happens fast, in fractions of seconds, and the carbon dioxide is expelled after a person exhales. In the meantime, the blood rich in oxygen returns, entering the person's heart. In short, the role played by breathing is that of keeping the concentration of oxygen high and carbon dioxide low within the alveoli.

169.   The diaphragm reduces, moving _____ in order to generate force at the thorax or chest cavity. This increases the thorax's volume, letting air rush inside the lungs.

The correct answer is: C) Downward

A person's diaphragm is a tough muscle that is, nevertheless, thin, and responsible for separating the thorax from the abdomen. It also happens to be domed in an upward direction when it is relaxed; therefore, when contracting, it begins to flatten out, leading to an increase in thoracic volume.

Considering that the pressure within a person's thorax is not as high as that of the atmosphere, air is bound to rush into the lungs, allowing the exchange of gases. As the wall of the chest expands, the primary muscle associated with respiration is the diaphragm. The muscles of the chest have a tinier part to play as far normal or conventional respiration is concerned.

170.   The diaphragm recovers its domed figure when it relaxes. The act brings about a rise in thoracic force that pushes the air from the person's lungs. Force at the thorax is required to increase over _____ pressure in order to ensure air is pushed from the lungs.

The correct answer is: B) Atmospheric

In order to eject air from the lungs, the prevailing transthoracic pressure has to increase, exceeding the pressure in the atmosphere or barometric pressure. The diaphragm relaxes and forms an upward dome, and then the intercostal muscles contract and pull a person's rib cage inward. This is a move that raises the transthoracic pressure so that it exceeds the barometric pressure that ends up pushing out the air.

171.   What ventilation technique has higher chances of yielding the minimal tidal volume?

The correct answer is: A) One-person bag-valve-mask

When mouth-to-mouth and mouth-to-mask are the ventilation techniques being used, maintaining a tight seal with the mouth of the patient is relatively easy, and this enables the delivery of sufficient tidal volume. Similarly, the two-person bag-valve-mask technique is dedicated to a single rescuer so that there is assurance of sufficient mask seal. In the meantime, the second rescuer squeezes the available ventilation bag using both hands, enabling delivery of sufficient tidal volume.

A single person using the bag-valve-mask often proves difficult since that one rescuer has to manually maintain an air passage, ensure the mask's seal is adequate and also simultaneously squeeze the bag.

172.   To help with intubation, a paramedic could make use of Sellick's maneuver, a procedure where the cartilage being compressed is the _____.

The correct answer is: A) Cricoid cartilage

Every one of the given structures is located within the same area, but what the paramedic makes use of is the cricoid cartilage. The choice of this cartilage stands out because the cricoid cartilage is the sole cartilage that can be considered a 'full ring.'

173.   You are transporting an elderly man experiencing respiratory distress and who been diagnosed in the past with COPD.

The unwell male has very light breathing that is fast with slight chest-wall movement as well as minor wheezing at the higher lung fields. Working with this condition, your arterial CO_2 intensity expectations would be?
The correct answer is: D) Elevated.

The patient can end up being hypercapnic because there is a probability his ventilation is just dead space. In such a case the patient's breaths will not be sufficiently deep to have air exchanges occurring within the alveoli, and so he will have heightened carbon dioxide levels.

174. You are transporting an ailing 48-year-old man from one medical facility to another. From the past record, you notice the man fell while working which led to his hip fracture as well as a head injury. At the moment, the man is going through labored inhalation of 30 per minute which has gradually become worse over the past day. The heart's frequency is 104, while blood pressure is 98/70. On listening, you notice diffuse rales on auscultation. The patient refutes pain experiences apart from the ones in relation to falling not so long ago. The greatest source of his respiratory pain would be?

The correct answer is: D) Adult respiratory distress syndrome.

Adult respiratory distress syndrome (ARDS) has to do with pulmonary edema which is not cardiogenic, presenting within a period ranging from 12 to 72 hours after a person has surgery or is injured. Congestive heart failure, as well as cardiogenic shock, begin with a compromise of a cardiac nature, although they also sometimes emerge from ARDS. As for flash pulmonary edema, its onset is rapid, and the situation can deteriorate over a period as short as half an hour. The condition is also linked to renal dysfunction.

175. The best method when it comes to administering ventilations to a patient who is apneic is _____.

The correct answer is: A) Two person bag-valve-mask.

The two-person bag-valve mask is the best method of ventilation administration. Nevertheless, it cannot always be assumed to be practical in field situations because resources are often limited, including space. Using a mouth-to-mask is also considered viable as a kind of artificial ventilation, yet there is a risk involving cross contamination when it comes to mouth-to-mouth ventilation. That risk makes health-care providers prefer the method less.

176. You arrive at an emergency scene and notice it seems like a domestic argument is going on regarding molestation of a child. You want to ask a child who is 5 years old about habits of elimination. Identify the word that would be most appropriate to use.

The correct answer is: A) 'Pee-Pee.'

A child of 5 years of age cannot understand what urination or micturation or deltrusion are, and as such, the most appropriate term for such circumstances is 'pee-pee.' This situation exemplifies situations where EMTs and other paramedics are required to correlate patient development with knowledge of communicating in an effective manner.

177.   If you are put in charge of designing a deployment plan for ambulances within the EMS system in your own community, and you are aiming at minimizing response time even as you utilize every available resource in the most efficient, cost-effective manner possible, which piece of information from the choices provided below would you consider of utmost value?

The correct answer is: B) The time and the location involving of the previous five years' calls

It is important to establish the most recent five years' call times and locations since the analysis could reveal certain patterns that will help delegate resources for emergency services appropriately. If, for instance, it is noted there are several car collisions in the morning hours when there is a rush, more units could be sent to particular strategic spots to make them easily available and ready to attend to potential incidents.

Also, the volume of calls and time can be reflective of a location's status in the socioeconomic sense, although that criterion on its own should not be used to determine resource allocation. Data on past collisions involving ambulances is crucial and ought to be utilized in minimizing such collisions, but it is not the best basis for ambulance allocations. As far as population age is concerned, it provides a bigger picture regarding the particular community's medical care needs, yet it cannot serve as the best basis for determining ambulance deployment.

178.   Which statement associated with continuous education does the public most value?

The correct answer is: D) It serves as a chance for EMTs to learn new and changing skills as well as about medications.

Medicine is a profession that is always evolving, and EMTs and other medical personnel need to keep abreast of information on current medications and techniques. Whereas it is correct to say EMS boards and EMTs' national registry define pre-requisites for continuous education for an EMT to remain certified, these aren't very relevant reasons to any community. The community is more interested in EMTs and paramedics being abreast of how to assess and treat emergency victims in the best way possible.

179.   Your call is to an industrial compound in a neighborhood where an incident is linked to potentially hazardous material. You are immediately informed that the number of employees affected is around 30 and also that there are many whom fumes have affected.

The team responsible for dealing with hazardous materials has been sent out, and it is estimated it will arrive at the emergency scene 20 minutes after the accident.

On reaching the scene, you find a worker at the entrance who informs you of the apparent contamination source, which is a huge white tank. There is a symbol, "NFPA 704" with several colors, and within a bluish diamond '4' is written. In a red diamond, '1' is written, and another diamond that is yellow. A white diamond contains no number.

A crowd approaches and informs you they have been exposed to some fluid that leaked from the huge tank. What action should you immediately take?

The correct answer is: C) Instruct those patients to get rid of their clothes and then rinse them using water.

Considering the particular substance that is the subject of contamination is known, there is no need to waste time before beginning decontamination. Water is universally accepted as the solution for decontamination, and hence there is no point in wasting time before starting to rinse off the potential contaminant. Once the workers have removed their outer clothing, they will have reduced their contamination.

It is not reasonable to have contamination victims await the specialized team for decontamination before you start your operations. At the same time, the team in charge of decontamination should not put their safety in jeopardy even when assessing the patients physically or taking their vital signs. Even though weak bleaching solutions are fine to use in some instances to decontaminate, the best of all solutions for that purpose is water in cases where it is not known exactly what the agent of contamination is.

180.   An EMT would benefit most from stress management following a critical incident such as the

The correct answer is: A) Demise of a four-year-old boy following a bad fall

Any child's death is a good reason to have the EMT or other involved paramedics require CISM (Critical Incident Stress Management) services. Also, a co-worker's demise or a serious threat to a co-worker may call for attention from CISM.

However, it is of utmost importance to recognize stress and identify coping abilities (or lack thereof), as opposed to simply involving CISM.

181.   If you release a patient's information to a newspaper and the patient considers that slander and sues you, what particular area of the statute could that patient's suit be based on?

The correct answer is: C) Tort

As for slander, it is not taken to be relevant under criminal law, and though constitutional, as well as federal laws, apply, the best answer is 'tort' as it is the one broadly applicable across all U.S. states. The law of tort solves differences involving individuals, and the issue in this question where someone discloses things pertaining to a person without that person's prior consent is a good example.

182.   What would you say is the importance of EMTs and other paramedics completing a checklist of equipment as every shift begins?

The correct answer is: B) Completing such a list minimizes liability risk linked to the provision of pre-hospital medical care.

Completing a checklist of supplies makes it convenient for EMTs to establish how prepared the ambulance team is to provide care to patients. The list provides an indication of whether every necessary supply and equipment is present and in good working order, as well as the respective expiration dates for medications in the ambulance. Completing the checklist minimizes liability linked to the provision of emergency care in the field by ascertaining that all that is required for proper caregiving to patients is readily available and in good order.

Missing supplies, malfunctioning equipment and expired drugs are some of the sources of potential liability particularly in cases linked to inappropriate care for a patient. However, the Occupational Safety and Health Administration, as well as the country's Department of Health & Human Services, do not demand health-care agencies maintain any equipment or supply checklists. Even insurance agencies never demand any of the teams submit such checklists for the sake of providing coverage of liability.

183.   You are your service's quality assurance committee's head. As you carry out a review of patient health-care reports before handing them in to your medical director, you notice a narrative indicating the patient had no bowel movements and also that he had had pain in the abdomen for a period of around three weeks. It is also documented that the patient had a fever that morning and took Tylenol tablets before experiencing nausea. What would be your advice to the relevant paramedic based on the report?

The correct answer is: D) Make use of a dictionary in confirming the spelling of words you are unsure of before doing your documenting.

It is important to spell properly when conducting documentation for emergencies away from the hospital. Any documentation with spelling errors does not look professional and can cause doubt regarding the quality of health care which was provided. As such, it is great when paramedics utilize dictionaries. The EMT-Basic document for advanced care is not suitable. Nevertheless, having an EMT read through the written document and point out spelling errors is not appropriate. Also, if someone creates abbreviations to represent words they are not sure how to spell, this could end up creating even more confusion. Documentation of only the patient-care aspects that an EMT is assured of spelling correctly means documentation would be incomplete and as such, inappropriate.

184.   The rules governing the behavior of EMT professionals are:

The correct answer is: B) Ethics

Ethics can be described as rules governing the conduct of professionals, while morals are perceptions individuals have regarding what is considered right or wrong. Standards and codes are not relevant where this question is concerned.

185.   Soon after arriving at a residence in the neighborhood you hear three sounds like gunshots. What immediate action should you take?

The correct answer is: D) Abandon the emergency scene until the police have secured it.

In case you find yourself at a dangerous site, you should leave that area in your ambulance and then notify the police or other law enforcement in order to have the area secured. Even though dispatch, as well as officers in charge of maintaining law and order, are to be informed, your first priority should be to ensure your own safety.

186.   You arrive at a scene where a vehicle has hit a tree, and the driver is slumped unconscious over the car's steering wheel as fire rages, burning the vehicle. You can even see fire in the passenger area. What is your first priority?

The correct answer is: D) Begin by taking care of your own safety and your partner's.

Whereas each of the answers given is a priority, in this case, your own safety and that of your team members should always be given the highest priority. After this, the next thing to focus on is extrication and patient management while paying continuous attention to the site in case the situation suddenly worsens.

187.   You have just released care of child suspected to be a victim of abuse to the hospital's emergency department. While discussing the situation with the crew from another ambulance, you are overheard by a family member saying the mother of the child is the most likely perpetrator of the abuse. What might you legally be accused of?

The correct answer is: D) Slander.

Slander is used in reference to an injury someone's personal character suffers, meaning the person's name or reputation, through the release of information that is false or shared with malicious intention. Slander also involves statements made recklessly without regard to the truth. If you wrote down such statements, they would constitute libel. As for negligence, it constitutes deviating from the level of care considered standard. Malfeasance is used in reference to negligence that involves performing an illegal or deliberately erroneous act.

188.   In the CQI programs, where the abbreviation stands for 'continued quality improvement, one of the options below is not included in the EMS system. Which is it?

The correct answer is: B) Gathering statistics involving the volume of calls and profiles of patients as well as skills employed

The advantages of a Continuous Quality Improvement program that is properly run on behalf of an EMS are more than just helpful to evaluate the performance of the system. Such a program enables data collection for the sake of conducting statistical analysis. It offers a way of establishing and addressing any weaknesses the system has and provides checks and balances. It also makes it easy to determine the kind of courses for continuous education to offer since case studies based on calls are very interesting.

However, these programs should not be involved in developing or implementing recourses to be used as punitive measures in areas where needed improvements are identified. If that happened, health-care providers would, very likely, be tempted to conceal any weaknesses discovered in the system, which is possible to do by falsifying individual patient reports. Some EMTs, apprehensive about highlighting concerns to management, might be among those writing inaccurate reports.

189.   As you compile a report pertaining to the patient, you note down that your patient was intoxicated and deliberately uncooperative. Such statements of a subjective nature can expose you to a legal suit involving:

The correct answer is: B) Libel

'Libel' is used in reference to the action of injuring someone's character by the use of written statements. Once you document an opinion of a personal or derogatory nature, it exposes you, as the EMT, to libel. Slander resembles libel with the difference being that slander is used in reference to statements that are false or malicious but of a verbal nature. As for malfeasance, it is used in reference to breach of duty due to performing an unlawful act. Res ipsa loquitur is used to refer to a doctrine of a legal nature used to support claims of negligence.

190.   The agency charged with regulation of EMS radio communication is:

The correct answer is: A) The Federal Communications Commission (FCC)

The FCC is charged with controlling and regulating every piece of non-governmental communication conveyed by radios within the U.S.

The National Highway Traffic Safety Administration (NHTSA) is an agent of the government charged with developing curriculum for the EMS. As for the Federal Emergency Management System (FEMA), it is charged with responding to and managing disasters. The National Association of Emergency Medical Technicians (NAEMT) is a professional non-governmental body dedicated to EMS advancement.

191.   A young girl, nine years of age, has been hit by a vehicle and the police cannot get ahold of her parents. Once dispatched to the scene, what will enable you to offer her treatment?

The correct answer is: (C) Consent that is implied.

There is implied consent because it is assumed that a parent would like an EMT to assist the child; therefore there ought to be no delay in evaluating, treating and or transporting the child when the parents or guardians are not present.

192.   What would be the correct action to take at '123 Somewhere Road' where there is a woman who has been injured, but the door is opened by a man who informs you that it is not your business and you should leave?

The correct answer is: (C) Return to your ambulance and, after you drive a safe distance, call for help from the police.

In case you think the situation could be unsafe, you are supposed to wait for the police to come and help. EMTs shouldn't put themselves in harm's way.

193.   When an EMT treats a patient who has refused the treatment, which crime has he/she committed?

The correct answer is: (B) Battery

Battery occurs when you treat a patient without legal consent.

194.   Protecting oneself and the patient from transferring bodily fluids is referred to as _____.

The correct answer is: (B) Body substance isolation

Isolation of bodily substances involves isolating all substances like tears, feces, urine, blood, etc. of those patients that are undergoing medical treatments, especially the emergency ones in cases of patients with diseases like hepatitis or HIV, in order to reduce transmission of these diseases to a minimum.

195.   People who offer help to the injured are protected from legal suits by which law?

The correct answer is: (C) Good Samaritan law

In common-law, one can use the Good Samaritan law as defense in cases of torts arising from rescue attempts.

196.   Name the areas where ambulances face the most risks of collision.

The correct answer is: (C)Where there is an intersection.

Vehicles at intersections are likely to block the person operating the ambulance from seeing cars that are approaching. Also, cars that are moving towards the intersection at a time when lights are changing may refuse to halt and instead accelerate. In addition, there are vehicles that have been sitting at stoplights which may fail to pay attention and accelerate without even looking.

197.   Headlights aren't deemed important 'emergency warning lights.' When should they be used?

The correct answer is: (A) When moving along the road.

Emergency lights are usually undermined in areas with busy traffic. Where safety is important, headlights come in handy. Even in broad daylight, headlights make it possible for people to see ambulances. There are headlights that have been wired in such a way that they flash when other emergency lights have been switched on, thereby enhancing the distance that you can spot an ambulance.

198.   When responding to incidents involving hazardous materials, where are EMTs supposed to approach a scene from?

The correct answer is: (A) Upwind, uphill or upriver

In response to known hazardous material incidents, an emergency responder needs to move towards the scene from upwind, uphill and upriver. This prevents the worker from being exposed to the toxin.

199.   Name the zone that an EMS is supposed to be set in a hazardous material incident.

The correct answer is: (D) Cold zone.

Since EMS crews do not have protective equipment for operating in warm or hot zones, patients are required to undergo thorough decontamination before EMS takes over, without exception, because the risk of exposing oneself to hazardous materials is very high.

200.   When is it considered all right to transport patients directly from hot zones without having to undergo decontamination?

The correct answer is: (B) At no one time because, regardless of a patient's sickness, he/she must undergo decontamination.

Decontamination should never be skipped because the danger of exposing EMS teams as well as other health-care providers is very high to allow a patient not to be decontaminated. Most decontamination teams are able to handle life-threatening cases as the patients go through decontamination processes.

201.   After calling 'air medical services' for a victim who has been involved in an accident, the aircraft gets in touch with you five minutes after takeoff, asking for information about the landing zone. What should not be left out in the safety brief?

The correct answer is: (D) All of the above choices.

Obstructions interfering with approach and takeoff of aircrafts are crucial to report. Electricity lines are particularly significant since they are not visible in the air and therefore the air-medical team relies on the team that is at the scene to point out such information. The surface type is crucial in anticipation of dust, debris or grass which may become airborne at the time of landing. Reporting any high-tension electricity lines in the region is also equally crucial because they could be within the pattern of approach or takeoff.

202.   Which patient would be the best fit for air transportation from the scene?

The correct answer is: (D)A male, 55 years old, who has been involved in an accident caused by his speeding motorcycle crashing into a cement highway barrier.

Other than the case of the speeding motorcycle, the rest of the answers listed don't carry the risk of endangering multiple organs. Stings from bees, painful as they are, pose less risk so long as there is no sign of anaphylaxis.

203. On arrival at the facility where patients are received, you have to transfer care to emergency department staff. This task is handled by the duty nurse, using a report indicating the medical history, an assessment of the patient's complaints and interventions in order to allow for_____?

The correct answer is: (A) Care to continue

Issuing a report to the staff at the receiving facility facilitates the continuation of care which not only allows for speedy responses by that institution but also eliminates unnecessary repetitive evaluations and assessments.

204. The EMTs in charge inform dispatch of their arrival at an accident scene involving several cars and explain their findings. "We are at the scene of an accident involving three cars. The patients are not in the cars but are walking around." This information is referred to as?

The correct answer is: (C) Scene size-up

There are several items that are required in a scene-size up:1) Inform dispatch of what might happen after the addition of more resources. 2) Prepare other medical teams for what they will find at the scene. 3) Downgrading/upgrading of assignments as necessary.

205. On arrival at a scene, which action is of utmost importance by the EMT?

The correct answer is: (C) Squad positioning for scene protection.

Whichever scene it is, safety is the number-one concern for emergency responders. Squad positioning to block traffic enables responders to safely carry on their duties within the scene. The vehicle should be parked in such a way that it can be accessed easily but does not compromise the safety of the scene.

206. To willfully leave a patient who is in need of care without a signed or verbal refusal of care is _____?

The correct answer is: B) Considered abandonment

The term 'abandonment' is used in reference to situations where continuing health care is required yet the patient's relationship with the EMT is terminated even when that patient has not refused care or transfer.

207. Which statement about disposable gloves is correct?

(E) The correct answer is: C) You can protect yourself and your patient from disease transmission by wearing gloves.
Gloves provide you and the patients with protection, and so most protocols today advise EMTs to make sure they wear them whenever coming into contact with patients. To remove used gloves, pull them off so they turn inside out as that ensures you cannot touch any part of the soiled surface. Every time you are dealing with a new patient you need to use fresh gloves.

208. EMTs wear 'High Efficiency Particulate Air' respirators (HEPA) whenever the patients they engage with have :

The correct answer is: B) Tuberculosis

HEPA respirators are worn when patients have airborne infections such as tuberculosis.

HIV and AIDS, as well as Hepatitis B, do not fall into that category as their pathogens are bloodborne. An open wound's contaminants are also considered to be bloodborne.

209. In which of the following situations should you call for immediate assistance?

The correct answer is: A) When you have two gunshot-wound patients to care for and they are in critical condition

You need to call for help when you have two or more patients whose conditions are critical. In this case, each of the two patients has gunshot wounds and require attention immediately, and for that reason, you should summon backup.

210. As you near a scene with potentially hazardous material, one way of identifying hazards is:

The correct answer is: C) Using binoculars to scan from a safe distance.

Do not take chances by entering a scene you think is contaminated. You need to make use of binoculars in surveying that scene while still a safe distance away so that you can identify any placards indicating dangerous material on-site. It is advisable to assume all victims, as well as bystanders, are contaminated and take precautionary measures.

211. Once medical direction issues orders, the very first thing you should do is:

The correct answer is: B) Repeat those orders to confirm what you heard

For the sake of avoiding misunderstandings, make a point of repeating medical instructions or orders precisely as you hear them. When you complete this, you can always question whatever order you are not sure about, and once you have completed a written patient health-care report, you need to include the order into the report.

212. Which option shows appropriate communication involving a patient?

The correct answer is: C) When the patient is a 75-year-old female: "Madam, in our opinion you need to be checked at the hospital just to ensure you are fine. Would you mind coming with us?"

It is important to speak in a respectful manner to every patient irrespective of whether that patient is intoxicated or not, or mentally impaired or not. Also, as you speak to a young child, it is important that you take into account that child's level of development.

213. What procedure would you consider correct in handling a used adjunct airway?

The correct answer is: A) Dispose of it by throwing it into a hazardous waste container.

The procedure most commonly followed involves safely disposing of used adjunct airways.

214. As for the right of a patient to reject care, the correct statement is:

The correct answer is: B) A mature patient with a sound mind who is also able to understand consequences has the right to reject treatment.

A person who is an adult and who is of sound mind has the right to reject treatment, although it is the duty of the EMT in charge to explain in in clear terms what the consequences are. The EMT should document any rejection of treatment in writing.

215. The importance of incident management systems is because they:

The correct answer is: C) Are an orderly communication method that can help in making decisions

Incident management systems comprise procedures which are contained in a system that is well-coordinated, enabling smooth operations at the scene of an emergency.

216. When it comes to patient/EMT confidentiality, it is correct that:

The correct answer is: D) It is necessary for your patient to sign a written release to enable the disclosure of confidential information. Otherwise, you cannot release it.

The only time you can freely release information pertaining to a patient is if that patient has signed a consent form.

217. In order for handwashing to be effective, it should take a minimum of:

The correct answer is D) 10 to 15 seconds

Rubs your soapy hands vigorously for 10 to 15 seconds. After such scrubbing, you can rinse off the soap with running water.

218. You need to put on a mask and eye protection whenever:

The correct answer is: B) You are beginning patient suctioning

Wearing a mask as well as having your eyes protected in instances when there is much room for splattering is important, and a good example is during suctioning.

219. Which situation below represents implied consent?

The correct answer is: D) When you offer an unconscious man life support after he was found by strangers.

Consent is described as 'implied' when you are supposed to treat the patient as if that patient has given consent, only this time the patient, though an adult, is not in a position to provide that consent.

220.   If you have a patient who cannot communicate in English, the best thing to do is:

The correct answer is: C) Try and contact a person capable of interpreting, such as a relative or a bystander.

Any time you have a patient not capable of communicating in English, you need to make an effort to find an interpreter, while taking care neither you nor the patient is misunderstood. It is a good idea to communicate in signs as well as gestures until a suitable interpreter is found.

Made in the USA
Coppell, TX
10 August 2020